ANIMAL RIGHTS

EDWARD F. DOLAN, JR.

Franklin Watts
New York/London/Toronto
Sydney/1986

A GROLIER COMPANY

ANIMAL RIGHTS

Photographs courtesy of:
© 1980, © 1981 Mary Bloom: pp. 12, 88; PETA:
pp. 30, 54, 56, 71, 128; Animal Welfare Institute:
pp. 31, 91; AP/Wide World: pp. 71 (inset), 83;
© 1984 Greenpeace/Rinehart: p. 84; © Len Rue,
Jr./Photo Researchers: p. 108; UPI/Bettmann
Newsphotos: p. 121.

Library of Congress Cataloging-in-Publication Data
Dolan, Edward F., 1924-
Animal rights.
Bibliography: p.
Includes index.
Summary: Surveys legislation, public attitudes, and
conditions in the area of treatment of animals,
particularly in scientific experimentation and also
in agriculture, hunting, and entertainment.
1. Animals, Treatment of—Law and legislation—United
States—Juvenile literature.   2. Animal experimentation—
Law and legislation—United States—Juvenile literature.
3. Animals, Treatment of—Law and legislation—Juvenile
literature.   4. Animal experimentation—Law and legislation—Juvenile literature.   [1. Animals—Treatment.
2. Animal experimentation]   I. Title.
KF3841.Z9D65 1986   346.7304'7   86-9291
ISBN 0-531-10247-5   347.30647

CONTENTS

Acknowledgment

The author and publisher wish to thank
Dan Mathews of People for the Ethical
Treatment of Animals for reviewing
the manuscript of this book and making
many valuable editorial suggestions.

ANIMAL RIGHTS

CHAPTER ONE

ANIMAL RIGHTS

The sun is rising in Asia. A farmer drops a heavy wooden yoke across his steer's neck. Rope lines run back from the yoke to a plow. The farmer takes his place at the plow and flicks the lines. Head down, the steer moves forward and starts a long day of readying a field for planting.

The golden retriever lies on the front porch of the suburban home in a midwestern state. He stretches lazily in the autumn sunshine as a man and woman come out of the house. They call to the dog, pet him gently, and set off on their customary late afternoon stroll, talking to him as they go along and now and again tossing a ball that he happily catches in midair. At the end of the walk, a full meal will be waiting for him.

CONTRASTS

These two examples from everyday life point out a very basic fact in the story of how we humans have lived with the animals around us down through the ages. They show that the story of human–animal relationships has always been one of sharp contrasts.

On the one hand, realizing that we are the most intelligent creatures on earth, we long ago came to regard animals as our inferiors and thus felt entitled to use them as servants. Ever since, they have been made to work for us in any manner that we have found helpful. They have pulled our wagons, carriages, and plows. They have helped us hunt down other animals for food or sport. They have entertained us in circuses and zoos, on motion picture and television screens, and in sporting contests ranging from horse and dog racing to deadly bullfighting and cockfighting. They have served as test subjects in experiments that have brought us some of our most important—and also some of our most insignificant and useless—scientific discoveries.

On the other hand, we have loved and cherished them as domesticated pets. They have given us companionship. They have shown us faith and love. They have provided the only contact with another living creature for many a lonely person.

And there is a further contrast. Many of us have treated animals with love and kindness, no matter whether they have been servants or pets. Many owners of work animals, for example, have never failed to tend them carefully. They have made certain that the animals are well fed, that they receive a proper amount of rest, and that their ills and work sores are treated with balms and medicines.

But many of us—again, regardless of whether the animals have been servants or pets—have treated them with anything from carelessness to outright cruelty. Animals undergoing scientific experiments have been cut open without first being given anesthetics. Pets have been abandoned and allowed to fend for themselves.

Guardian of the home, this golden
retriever dog stands with boot in
mouth, awaiting its owner.

They have been thoughtlessly left in closed cars on hot days and have died of the heat. They have been beaten or cruelly treated in countless other ways. In early 1985, the people of Oregon were shocked to learn that a fifteen-year-old boy had obtained kittens from an animal shelter and had fed them to his pet boa constrictor. The people of New York State were just as shocked when, later in the year, they read of the vandals who threw a firebomb into an animal shelter and caused a fire in which sixty animals perished.

SUBJUGATION AND RESPONSIBILITY

While it is true that these sharp contrasts are basic facts in the age-old story of human–animal relationships, they do no more than point to a still more basic fact, the most basic one of all: Regardless of whether our treatment has been loving or abusive, we humans have subjugated the animals around us to our needs, that is, we have made them meet our needs *regardless of their own needs and natures.*

Where their natures have called for them to roam free, often we have put them in harnesses to help with our work or have enclosed them in backyards, houses, or cages to fulfill our desire for companionship. As the human population has multiplied through the centuries, we have encroached on areas that were hitherto animal domains; we have built our homes, factories, and stores there and have driven the animals out. These encroachments, along with our need for food and the joy that some of us take in hunting for sport, have threatened some animal species with extinction and have totally eradicated others. To keep the animal population in control as ours has grown, we have curtailed their natural bent to reproduce themselves; we have done so by such means as spaying and neutering. In our need to protect ourselves from disease and in our desire to learn more about our world, we have ignored the fact that animals can feel pain, as we have made them the subjects of medical and scientific experimentation.

On the other hand, we have not been totally blind to their needs and natures. Since the most ancient times, despite the mistreatments listed above, we have felt certain responsibilities toward animals. In the main, we have considered it our duty to safeguard their welfare. Knowing that they will sicken and die without food, we have fed them. Understanding that they can feel physical pain and sensing that they have emotions, we have considered it a basic duty to treat them with kindness.

This compassion has most often been seen in those decent ways that countless humans have treated their work animals and pets through the centuries. It has also been seen in the concerned groups and individuals who have taken a stand against the animal abuse that has occurred throughout those very same centuries. For example, Christian and Jewish scholars have long objected to abuse by arguing that the ancient laws of their religions, while not containing specific rules regarding animal treatment, imply that kindness is mandatory. Consequently, it should always be shown by people who look on themselves as good Jews or Christians. The kindly treatment of animals is also an ancient precept in certain Eastern religions, such as Hinduism and Buddhism. These Eastern religions, along with many ancient Greek and Roman philosophers—among them Pythagoras and Plutarch—early advocated the practice of vegetarianism (the eating of only nonmeat products) as a kindness towards animals and as an effective means of maintaining good health. Thinkers in both ancient times and the Middle Ages debated whether animals have souls and thus have as much a right to compassionate treatment as humans. They never agreed on an answer.

In a period closer to our own times, the leaders of the Massachusetts Bay Colony in 1641 enacted a law forbidding the citizens to treat their animals cruelly. It was the first animal protection law in North America. Little more than a century later—in 1776—a British cleric named Humphrey Primatt spoke out against animal cruelty with words that remain a battle cry for compassion to this day: "Pain is pain, whether it is inflicted on man or beast."

The nineteenth century saw the formation of humane and antivivisection societies in a number of countries, the United States and Great Britain among them. The humane societies spoke out against the cruelties of animal owners and built shelters for strays and homeless pets. The antivivisection societies, as their names made clear, opposed the vivisection—the cutting open of live animals—in the scientific laboratories of the day. These groups continue their work today in various parts of the world. In North America, they are represented by such organizations as the Canadian Federation of Humane Societies, the American Humane Association, the Humane Society of the United States, and the American Society for the Prevention of Cruelty to Animals. Of the U.S. groups, the oldest are the Society for the Prevention of Cruelty to Animals and the American Humane Assocation. The former was founded in 1866, and the latter in 1877.

In the United States, the nineteenth century also saw the enactment of the first state and federal animal protection laws. The first state law was passed in New York State in 1826. It made the mistreatment of horses, cattle, and sheep a misdemeanor. The law, however, applied only to *owned* animals; strays and homeless animals were left unprotected.

The rest of the states passed anticruelty laws of their

own throughout the remainder of the 1800s and into the twentieth century. In general, these measures resembled the New York law in that they imposed misdemeanor fines on owners who mistreated their work animals and pets. More severe penalities, such as those given for harming a human being, were not imposed (and are still not imposed today) because the animals were regarded as inferior to humans. Some states extended the penalties to cover abuses in pet stores and pounds. A number of states, at the vigorous urging of the American Humane Association and fellow groups, enacted legislation against cruel methods of branding cattle.

At the federal level, the first anticruelty law took shape in 1873. Called the Twenty-Eight-Hour Law, it came into being when Congress learned of the terrible and exhausting conditions under which cattle, swine, and sheep were transported by rail and ship to meat centers for slaughtering prior to being marketed. The law required the animals to be rested and given food and water every twenty-eight hours.

Next, in 1885, U.S. Senator George F. Hoar of Massachusetts led a campaign that resulted in the states banning the killing of birds for the purpose of using their plumage to decorate dresses and hats.

The latter half of the twentieth century saw two additional animal laws go into the federal books. The first was targeted at the cruel manner in which food animals were slaughtered for marketing. Without the use of any pain-killing measures, the doomed animals were suspended by one leg from a rope or chain and were then axed to death. Taking action against the practice, Congress passed the Humane Slaughter Act of 1958. The Act required that the animals be stunned before being killed.

The expanding work of science in the twentieth century triggered the second law. Science was exploring ever deeper into its many fields. New products were being developed and had to be tested before they could be safely sold to consumers. Likewise, an increasing number of new medical drugs were under development and test. The result: an awesome number of animals were being recruited for laboratory experimentation (it is estimated that some 200 million animals are used today in the world's labs). The humane societies were stunned by the number alone. And they were infuriated by many reports of the suffering that the animals were made to endure before, during, and after experimentation. At the insistent urging of the societies, Congress passed the Animal Welfare Act in 1966. In the coming pages, we'll talk more of the Act and the exact sufferings of the lab animals. For now, let us simply say that the Act demands an improvement in their living conditions and, under certain circumstances, requires that they be given pain-killers.

ANIMAL RIGHTS

And so the concern for the welfare of animals has always been great and has always been present to combat the cruelties shown them by far too many humans. Since the mid-1970s, that concern has been greater than ever before.

Much responsible for the increased worry is Peter Singer, a professor of philosophy at the Australian National University and the author of the book, *Animal Liberation*. In the book, which was first published in 1975, Singer reported on the animal sufferings endured at human hands in all walks of life. He then drove home the point that the exploitation of animals—their use for human needs while their own needs and natures are ignored—has the same basis as human slavery. In comparing their exploitation to human slavery, Singer left no doubt that he believed they had as much right as a human not to be unfairly imprisoned.

Further, Singer invented a new word in his book—*specieism,* meaning that animals are often mistreated not because they are regarded as our servants or inferiors but because they are of a different species than ours. Basically, the term means for animals what racism and sexism mean for humans. Racism and sexism can harm the peoples towards whom they are directed and can often deprive the victims of many rights and privileges. Specieism does the same kind of injury to animals.

The Singer book led to two important developments in the field of animal welfare. First, because it was published in a number of countries, it aroused the sympathy of countless people who had never really thought about the suffering. They began to join the ranks of those already working to help the animals. The press and television, sensing the rising interest in animal matters, reported on what both the new and veteran advocates were doing and on the cruelties they were finding. In a short time, the suffering of the animals became what it is today—a major issue for civilized people in North America, Europe, and Australia.

Second, in discussing specieism and comparing animals to human slaves, the book gave a new direction to the regard felt for the animals. Hitherto, the concentration had been on animal welfare. But now people began to think in terms of *animal rights.* The attitude had always been that we humans are obligated to treat animals with compassion because we are superior to them. Now, however, we were forced to the question: are we obliged to be compassionate not only because we are the superior species but also because the animals, as fellow living creatures and sharers of the planet with us, have the *right* to decent treatment?

In the minds of the people advocating decency towards animals, the answer is yes. Adding to the impact of the Singer book were the many new facts that studies of animal life were bringing to light. We were learning more and more about the nature of animals and finding that, in their own ways, they are as sensitive, as emotional, and as caring of their young as we. And we were learning more and more about animal behaviors, behaviors that revealed many animals to be more intelligent than we had once thought, that showed some to be capable of maintaining complex societies, and that astonished us with indications that many species had developed the means of voice communication. There was even the possibility that we would one day be able to communicate verbally with some species. All this supported Singer's position that animals, as fellow living creatures and sharers of the planet, are indeed entitled to many of the rights held by humans.

THE RIGHTS THEMSELVES

Just what rights do animals hold? This question can best be answered by first pointing out the rights that they are felt not to hold. Animals, of course, do not hold the right of free speech for the simple reason that they never developed the complex speech patterns of humans and so have no need for it. Nor—except for such animals as fish, birds, and creatures in the wild—do they have the right to roam where they wish. Complete freedom, especially in crowded areas, is seen as unfair to humans and dangerous for both people and animals. Not even human beings are permitted to go wherever some whim might take them. To see the truth of this, try driving a car down the wrong side of the street.

Furthermore, it is felt that animals do not have the right to multiply freely. Unrestrained breeding can be a matter of unfair discomfort and heavy costs (for one, the cost of maintaining shelters for an overabundance of animals) for humans. And it can be a matter of danger to the animals: An overabundance of cats, for instance, can doom many of them to become strays faced with the hazards that always accompany homelessness—injury, illness, and starvation.

What, then, are the rights that the animals *do* hold? As animal advocates everywhere see them, they are the following:

The right to enjoy their lives according to what is called their *telos*—their basic natures. If they enjoy physical activity and affection, then they are entitled to sufficient exercise and play and to displays of our love for them. We may not force them to live in ways that are completely alien to their natures, penning them up at all times or ignoring them.

The right to good health. They are entitled to a proper diet and good medical care.

The right to comfort and the avoidance of pain. We cannot treat them cruelly or maintain them in unhealthy and uncomfortable living conditions. When they are in pain, we must look on them as we would a suffering human. We must do all possible to reduce their pain or eradicate it altogether.

The right to a humane death. When we kill animals for food or a scientific purpose, we must take all care to make that death as painless as possible. [Note: It must be pointed out that the killing of animals is a highly controversial point among animal advocates. As we'll see in later chapters, some advocates feel that it is necessary to kill animals for food; others believe that any killing whatsoever is wrong and urge that all people adopt vegetarianism as a way to spare the animals.]

The right to survival. We must not needlessly kill animals. And we must not drive them completely out of their wildlife domains and thus threaten them with extinction. A balance must be sought between the animal's need to survive and our need for space in which to establish homes and industries. The largest areas possible must be preserved for the animals.

Some animal advocates agree that these rights do not prohibit humans from using animals as we have always used them—as food, servants, and pets. Furthermore, some advocates believe that an effort to stop such uses would be impractical. People the world over are long accustomed to these uses, see many of them as necessary, and thus would not accept such a drastic change. Consequently, rather than alter what have always been fundamental human–animal relationships, the rights simply heighten our awareness of the kinds of treatment to which any animal is entitled as a co-inhabitant of the planet.

And so the move toward animal rights is seeking to help the animals to a better life while allowing certain of their traditional relationships with humans to continue. In all, the advocates are calling for everyone to treat animals with the same compassion that sensitive people have always shown them.

The following chapters will report on the efforts currently being made to achieve this end. In turn, we will look at what is being done to better the lot of animals everywhere and protect their rights as they perform what have long been their traditional services—as test subjects in scientific experiments; as providers of food and clothing in commerce; as entertainers in motion pictures, zoos, and the like; as competitors and prey in sports; and as pets in the home.

Let us now turn to the story of the animals used for scientific experiments. It is a story that can be divided into two parts: The first concerns the pain and death suffered in the experiments themselves; the second deals with the sorry conditions under which the animals often live before, during, and following experimentation. Heading the list of these conditions are the crowded and unsanitary housing provided by many labs and the insensitive and even cruel treatment given the animals by some researchers.

We will begin with the experiments.

CHAPTER TWO

ANIMALS FOR SCIENCE

Animals have been used in scientific research and experimentation for centuries. They have endured pain and death in the endless quest to unearth the secrets of the body, find effective medications and treatments for combating disease, devise improved surgical procedures, and develop new products for human consumption. Animals continue to suffer and die today in the name of human betterment as the quest goes on.

On several counts, science has long claimed that animals are necessary for successful laboratory work. For one, many a scientist sees them as vital to the study of human disease because, in a number of ways, they are biologically similar to people. Other scientists point to the age-old rule that prohibits humans from being forced to undergo experimentation. Human legal and moral rights make such experimentation impossible. (Note: There have been times in history, however, when experimentation was performed on slaves.) Consequently, many scientists say that, were it not for animals, painful laboratory experiments would have to wait for human volunteers. The wait could be a long one, slowing or even stopping many a valuable advance.

And so animals have been made to suffer and die in our place. The suffering and death are more widespread at present than ever before. By itself, the death rate is awesome. The Animal Protection Institute of America estimates that in the United States alone three laboratory animals die every second.

The suffering and death are so widespread today because scientific investigation has become such a broad field. Research laboratories can be found throughout the world. Furthermore, the variety of scientific experimentation today is wider than ever in the past. Experiments that were not even dreamed of at the opening of our century are now routinely undertaken every day of the week. Obviously, more animals than ever before are needed; worldwide, their number has reached a total that staggers the imagination.

THE ANIMALS

Just how staggering is that total? In his book *Animal Rights and Human Morality,* Professor Bernard E. Rollin of the College of Veterinary Medicine at Colorado State University writes that 200 million animals are employed worldwide each year in scientific research. He adds that 100 million of those animals are to be found in U.S. laboratories. Other estimates set the annual U.S. total at somewhere between 60 million and 90 million.

The animals make up a varied group: rats, mice, guinea pigs, dogs, cats, baboons, monkeys, cows, pigs, ponies, sheep, and even birds. Of all the laboratory animals, mice and rats are the ones most in demand. Professor Rollin writes that 50 million mice and 20 million rats are used in the United States annually. They account for 70 percent of all the animals that he says are used here. In great part, they are so popular because they are small and easy to handle. They are also popular because of their short gestation period (pregnancy) and their rapid sexual maturation.

Next in demand are dogs and cats. Professor Rollin estimates that each year American laboratories perform experiments on 450,000 dogs and 200,000 cats.

In the United States and elsewhere, animal experiments take place in all types of laboratories—in labs maintained by universities, medical schools, hospitals, junior and senior high schools, and food, cosmetics, and chemical companies. The experiments range from those intended to gain a greater understanding of the world about and beyond us to those that play a part in the basic education of our young people. In all, however, these varied experiments can be placed within six areas of research.

THE RESEARCH

The six areas are biological research, biomedical research, drug development, product testing, product extraction, and educational experimentation.

Biological Research
In this area researchers look into questions and theories on the nature of life and the functions of the human and animal body. Their aim is the gathering of "pure knowledge"—that is, knowledge acquired for the sake of knowing more about ourselves and our world—and they are not primarily concerned with what might be the practical applications of their findings.

Biomedical Research
Here scientists test questions and theories concerning the nature, cause, and possible cures of such problems as disease, genetic defects, birth defects, and abnormalities in the functions of the body. The current research

into the cause of the various cancers provides a major example of the work done in this category.

Drug Development

Just as the name suggests, work in this area is aimed at finding drugs that can be of value in treating, curing, or arresting various diseases and disorders. Developed and tested here are drugs for health problems ranging from such potentially fatal illnesses as cancer and heart disease to such minor but nevertheless troublesome ailments as hay fever and the common cold.

Product Testing

Before various consumer products—food additives, cosmetics, shampoos, skin conditioners, industrial chemical, herbicides, pesticides, and the such—can be marketed, the laws of the United States and other countries require that they be thoroughly tested to establish that they can be safely used by humans. The testing seeks to answer several questions: Is the product toxic (poisonous)? Will it prove to be a carcinogen (a substance able to induce cancer)? Will it show itself to be a teratogen (a substance that causes birth defects)? Will it damage the skin, eyes, or nasal passages?

Product Extraction

A number of animals have been found to contain products that fight illness and promote good health. Vitamin A, for example, comes from cod and other fishes. Vitamin E, which is also contained in wheat germ oil and cereals, can be extracted from egg yolks and beef liver. Many of the serums that physicians use to treat or immunize against various illnesses (in both humans and animals) are likewise extracted from animals. To mention just one, the serum employed against cholera comes from the horse.

The work in this area is divided between the extraction of known animal products and research aimed at discovering new products.

Educational Experimentation
This final area involves animals used in schools for various purposes—for demonstration, dissection, elementary and high school science projects, and surgical training in medical schools.

THE EXPERIMENTS

It would be an overstatement to say that every experiment performed in the six areas brings either pain or death, but a great number do bring one or the other or both—pain because some laboratories do not anesthetize the animals (in part, for fear that pain killers will alter the results of a test), and death because many experiments involve lethal substances or procedures. To see what all too often happens, we need only look at two experiments that have been routinely conducted worldwide for decades: the Draize and LD50 tests.

The Draize Test
The Draize test is a consumer-product test. It is meant to show whether a product planned for marketing will irritate the human eye. The test was developed during World War II when the United States assisted Great Britain in animal tests to ascertain the degree of eye irritation caused by gases being developed for chemical warfare.

The white rabbit proved to be especially useful in those tests because its eye does not have a tear duct, the passageway through which tears are able to escape. In the absence of the duct, the amount of tears induced by a gas could be more clearly seen and the degree of irritation more soundly judged. So successful did those first experiments seem to be that the Draize test became—

and remains to this day—the standard test internationally for determining the eye irritation caused by various products, especially cosmetics and shampoos. The white rabbit continues to serve as its subject animal.

Just how is the Draize test given? When a substance is to be checked, several white rabbits are placed in restraining gear and $1/10$ of a milliliter of the test substance is dropped into one eye of each rabbit; the other eye is left untested. Both eyes are then checked for comparison, with the tested eye being observed for such effects as redness, swelling, the amount of tears shed, and damage to the cornea. The number and severity of effects observed are recorded and scored over the span of a week. The test ends when the scores are compiled and averaged to arrive at an idea of how irritating the substance may be to the human eye.

That the Draize test is recognized as painful is seen in one fact: In the past the test was never conducted with the help of pain killers but now a growing number of labs are using a local anesthetic. Many scientists object to the anesthetic; they say that it may jeopardize the test's accuracy by reducing the production of tears and altering such reactions as blinking.

The LD50 Test
A primary goal in the testing of many consumer products is to discover just how toxic—poisonous—they may be to humans. A standard method worldwide for determining toxicity is the LD50 test, which is the abbreviation for *lethal dose 50 percent*. The test has been used in laboratories since the late 1920s.

Determination of the LD50 is supposed to answer the following question: What is the amount of a product that, when given to a group of animals, will result in the death of half their number within 14 days? That amount is an indicator of the dangers posed for humans by the substance.

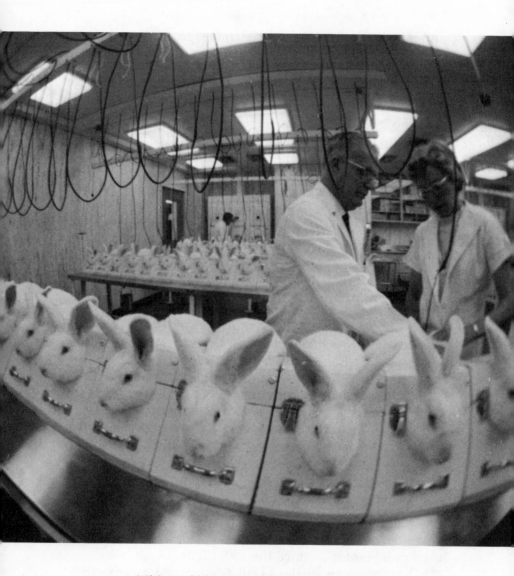

White rabbits undergoing the Draize test,
in which a substance is injected into
their eyes to see what degree of irritation
is caused. This test is used to determine
eye irritation caused by such
products as cosmetics and shampoos.

*A small creature is being given the LD50
(lethal dose 50 percent) test. The test
is supposed to answer the question, what
is the amount of a product that, when given
to a group of animals, will result in the death
of half their number within fourteen days?*

Rats, mice, cats, dogs, and especially rabbits are subjected to LD50 testing, with 40 to 200 being used at a time. In her book *Sharing the Kingdom: Animals and Their Rights*, Karen O'Connor writes that the test substances are given to the animals in various ways. Sometimes they are introduced via stomach tubes. Sometimes they are given in capsules, and sometimes are mixed into food. They cause a variety of reactions, among them diarrhea, vomiting, loss of appetite, and changes in the condition of the animal coats. The test, now more than fifty years old, is used in more than twenty countries.

WHY DON'T PEOPLE OBJECT?

Perhaps it is unfair to ask the question, Why don't people object to what is happening to the laboratory animals? As we all know, the fact is that increasing numbers of people *are* objecting now that the suffering and pain are coming to light. They are calling for changes. Still, mushrooming though it is, the outcry is not as strong as it might be. There are countless people who have yet to raise their voices in protest; furthermore, they may never do so. Why?

The answers are several. To begin, there is the fact that many laboratory animals are being used in the campaign to rid the world of its most feared diseases. As we will see later, animal advocates believe that this campaign could be waged just as successfully—and perhaps even more successfully—with the development of experiments not employing animals. Nevertheless, it is a campaign that is making great advances in understanding, treating, and perhaps one day curing or totally preventing such diseases as cancer in both humans and animals. And, were it not for the animal experiments performed long ago by such men as France's Louis Pasteur and Germany's Robert Koch, we would still be the helpless victims of hydrophobia (rabies), cholera, and tuberculosis. Everyone appreciates these many works and, in the minds of many people, the benefits to be won are worth far more than the costs in animal life.

Another answer stems from our age-old use of animals as servants. Since we have long felt entitled to have animals do everything from pull our wagons to act as targets in our hunting sports, far too many of us now feel scant concern about their use to help advance the cause of scientific research and testing.

Furthermore, we live in an era in which science is greatly respected. Considering the magnificent work that has been accomplished on all scientific fronts in our century alone, that respect is well deserved. But it is a respect that has led to a blind admiration in many people; so far as they are concerned, "anything goes"— including animal (and even human) pain and death—so long as it is done in the name of science. Our respect for science has also caused many of us to accept as complete truth the old claim that animals are necessary for successful research. As we will see in the next chapter, this claim—despite the significant animal research of Pasteur, Koch, and others—has always been *only partly true*. Still, countless people go on accepting it as gospel.

Next, we come to the fact that rats and mice are the laboratory animals most in demand. Neither species enjoys a happy reputation among humans. Historically, both have been associated with filth, disease, and plague. Many people find it impossible to feel revulsion at the suffering these small creatures endure in the laboratory. As a number of animal advocates have put it, things might be quite different if cute little kittens and puppies—or E.T., with all his extraterrestial charm— were the most used of the laboratory animals.

Aside from the lack of feeling for rats and mice, it must also be admitted that many of our fellow human beings are pretty unfeeling when it comes to *anyone's* pain—anyone else's pain, that is. They are unable to envision the degree of another's suffering by recalling the suffering that they themselves have experienced at one time or another, with the result that they think little of what is endured in the laboratory. It is simply a matter of lack of imagination.

Additionally, even the most imaginative of people can be—and often are—duped into insensitivity. Unless they stop to think, they can be easily fooled by the manner in which many scientists talk of animal experiments. The scientists are not likely to say that the animals suffer pain but, rather, that they "experience discomfort." Nor are they likely to say bluntly that the animals are killed; instead, the noble-sounding term *sacrificed* is used. All such words blunt the mind to the terrible realities of the situation.

A CHANGE OF DIRECTION

Despite all these answers—all these reasons for not caring about the animals—there is the growing outcry against what is happening in today's laboratories. Happily, it is an outcry that is bringing about a change of direction in the way in which scienfitic experiments have long been conducted. Animal advocates and the many concerned scientists who have joined their ranks are now working to develop new systems of experimentation that will spare the animals.

These new systems are known as alternative methods of experimentation, which is the subject of our next chapter.

CHAPTER THREE

ANIMALS FOR SCIENCE: ALTERNATIVES TO SUFFERING

As you know, science has long claimed that animals are necessary for success in the laboratory. The argument has been that they are vital because they are, in certain ways, biologically similar to people and because we humans cannot be made to undergo experiments. Our civil and moral rights protect us here.

— It is true that animals were once necessary for success in some laboratory works. A case in point is Louis Pasteur's study of hydrophobia in the late 1800s. Hydrophobia is the deadly disease that strikes when we are bitten by rabid animals. The French scientist infected dogs with the germs of rabies early in the series of experiments that led to his development of the vaccine now used to protect us from hydrophobia. Promising death, the experiments simply could not be tried on human volunteers, even if some foolhardy person had dared offer to help.

But it is also true that a great many scientific advances have been made without animal help. Friends of Animals, a U.S. advocate organization, points to seventeen examples in its booklet *Alternatives to Research on Animals*. This list, which the group says is far from complete, includes the discoveries of penicillin, insulin, radium, the thermometer, quinine, X ray, and the smallpox vaccine.

And so the claim has always been only partly true. Then why have some scientists insisted that the animals are so necessary? Many animal advocates think that it has been simply a matter of convenience. It has permitted the scientists to avoid the difficulties of finding animal-free ways of performing their experiments, difficulties that might delay their work.

ALTERNATIVES
TO SUFFERING

But things are changing. There are scientists everywhere who are deeply concerned about the rights and welfare of lab animals. The recent years have seen them begin to search for and develop alternative methods of experimentation, methods that, in time, can replace today's animal experiments.

Often called "nonanimal" methods, these alternatives are ways of performing experiments without animals or, in some cases, with the least number possible; most call for the use of other life forms. Some are built around such nonliving things as computers and dummies.

The search for these alternatives is being widely applauded. But this is not to say that it is admired everywhere. Some advocates feel that there is a better way to protect the animals—in fact, the only way—and that is to ban outright their use in the laboratory. Years, they argue, will be needed to find enough alternatives to replace *all* the experiments with animals, if indeed enough alternatives can ever be found. A ban would hurry matters along and save countless animal lives, and it would put an immediate end to many current experiments that animal advocates condemn as useless. We will explain and discuss these criticized experiments as we go along.

Just as many advocates, however, feel that a ban would not work. They believe it would do nothing but anger the public, because so many of today's lab animals are being used in the campaign to rid the world of its most feared diseases. Even though the alternative methods are beginning to replace the animal experiments, a ban would dry up what is still the prime source of test subjects and would undoubtedly delay some major discoveries and advances. The public would not tolerate the possiblity of such delays.

Consequently, the alternative methods are widely accepted as not only a good solution but the only feasible one as well—one that balances the welfare of the animals with the needs of the researchers. Modern scientific knowledge has made them possible and they are being put to increasing use with each passing year. This chapter will tell the story of their development. It is a story that begins with some doubts that many scientists have about certain of today's animal experiments.

TODAY'S METHODS: SOME DOUBTS

The search for alternative methods is not based solely on a concern for the laboratory animals; it is based also on the growing suspicion that many of today's experiments, especially those done with consumer products, provide useless results. Even though the lab animals are biologically similar to people, the experiments are suspected of producing effects in an animal that may well not apply to a human. If this is indeed the case, then such experiments are not only painful and lethal but also painful and lethal to no avail.

The reasons why the effects may differ between animals and humans are several and complex. At the base, however, they concern such matters as the test dosages given and the physical traits of the individual animals and species. Furthermore, although animals and humans are biologically similar, there are many ways in which they differ biologically from each other.

One test that is currently under fire because its results may be of no value to humans in the LD50. In finding the dosage that will kill 50 percent of the animal subjects, the researchers feed them large amounts of a product or a substance used in the product. Critics of the test argue that the heavy doses prove nothing about a product's dangers for humans, because, unless a suicide attempt or an accident is involved, people will not consume the tested substance in great amounts. Rather, it will be taken in small quantities over extended periods of time. The test tells the researchers nothing of the harm a substance may do when used under these circumstances. Also, many scientists and advocates fear that the animals often die not because they are given a substance that is itself dangerously toxic but because it is fed to them in too great an amount.

Doubts about the validity of such tests as the LD50—along with a deepened recognition of their cruelty—have done much to trigger the search for alternative methods of experimentation. Two alternatives are being sought: substitution and reduction.

SUBSTITUTION

Just as the term indicates, the goal here is to discover methods of testing that will see the animals replaced by substitute subjects. Much excellent work is being done in this area. For instance, biochemist Bruce Ames of the University of California at Berkeley has developed a test that replaces animals in the screening of chemicals that might cause cancer, mutations, or birth defects. Instead of exposing animals to the various chemicals, the test employs a special strain of bacteria called *Salmonella*.

The Ames test is now several years old. Early in its history, it revealed the carcinogenic potential of several hair dyes and uncovered the chemical hazards of a fire-retardant material that was widely used in children's sleepwear. The test exposed these chemical hazards more than a year before the U.S. Consumer Products Commission ordered the sleepwear (some 20 million garments) to be taken off the market at the start of the 1980s. The commission issued its order on the basis of animal testing.

The *Salmonella* bacteria of the Ames test are single-cell organisms (microorganisms). Other microorganisms are presently under study to see if they can be useful in experimentation, with many showing that they react to poisonous substances just as humans and animals do. One test under development with microorganisms is designed to reveal substances that cause birth defects. Hitherto, testing for birth defects has required the use of pregnant animals.

Single-cell organisms are the simplest of life forms. Even though they are living creatures, it is felt humane to substitute them for the lab animals. They do not have central nervous systems and thus are thought unable to feel pain.

Human and animal tissues are now being employed in some experiments. In one, doctors remove bits of cancerous tissue from a patient's body, nurture them in the laboratory, and then test them with the various drugs that might be used to treat the patient. The drug that works best is chosen and the ones that produce dangerous side effects are discarded. The test is superior to those that can be done with animals. The animal tests can give only a "general picture" of a drug's effects, because cancer cells differ from person to person. A drug that works for one patient might well not work for another. Only by using the patient's own cells can the most precise information on a drug's actions be obtained.

In another tissue experiment, chicken embryos are taking the place of the white rabbit's eye in a test that Dr. Joseph Leighton of the Medical College of Pennsylvania has devised as a possible substitute for the notorious Draize test. The embryos react in the same manner as the rabbit's eye. The experiment is painless, because nine-day-old embryos are used; they have no sensory nerve fibers at that time. Some researchers are looking into the use of chicken embryos to replace animals in experiments studying the action and spread of viruses.

Alternative methods involving computers are of particular interest to many scientists. It is felt that computers can be of excellent service in analyzing research data and predicting the properties and actions of new drugs. Researchers at Health Designs, Inc., in Rochester, New York, have devised a computer program that indicates dangerous chemicals in the early stages of testing and can be used as an alternative to the present LD50 test. Some researchers are working on computer programs that can simulate actions and reactions of animals.

Computers, of course, are nonliving substitutes. So are the dummies that have been developed for the study of traffic injuries. They are now being substituted for animals in the test crashes staged by automobile manufacturers in the search for safer car designs and new safety features. Likewise, dummies with realistic, working internal organs are replacing animals in the surgical training of doctors and nurses.

Human Substitutes

Many scientists, among them Dr. Richmond C. Hubbard, are recommending that human volunteers be increasingly employed in a number of research programs. Dr. Hubbard is the chairman of the Medical

Research Modernization Committee, a group of 650 health-care professionals who are studying and urging new methods of experimentation. In a letter written to *The New York Times* newspaper in 1985, he pointed out several research areas in which humans could serve better than animals.

He mentioned first the studies into the disease that is currently making headlines everywhere, AIDS (acquired immune deficiency syndrome). At present, attempts are being made to infect primates with AIDS so that they can serve as models in the development of a protective vaccine. Dr. Hubbard wrote that human research in AIDS is imperative, because it will take years for the animals to develop the disease—or, more precisely, an AIDS-like disease. Though the animal disease resembles human AIDS in some ways, there is no assurance that the two are exactly the same. (For example, human AIDS patients often develop a rare skin cancer, Kaposi's sarcoma, which has never been seen in primates with AIDS.) Consequently, years are going to be spent in the quest for a vaccine that may work well for animals but not for humans, and in the meantime humans will be dying of the disease. Obviously, the move toward a vaccine would be accelerated through a study of human victims. Dr. Hubbard remarked that there are surely human victims who would be willing to volunteer for the study; in the process they might save their own lives or those of future patients.

Dr. Hubbard then went on to list several other diseases that could be better studied with humans, including multiple sclerosis, intractable arthritis, and cancer.

REDUCTION

As in the case of substitiution, this term means exactly what it says. The aim is to reduce the number of animals sacrificed in laboratories.

Colin Muir, a pharmacologist at the Leicester Polytechnic Institute in England, has been working in this area and has devised a test to reduce the number of rabbits used in the Draize test. Rather than apply a substance to a rabbit's eye, Muir inserts it into the ileum, a sensitive portion of the intestine, of a freshly killed rabbit. The irritants in the substance prompt the ileum into spasms of various intensities. The spasms are sent by electrical signal to a polygraph. Muir's work with his test shows that the ileum reacts to irritants in the same way as the white rabbit's eye.

Muir hopes to see his procedure eventually replace the Draize test. While admitting that a rabbit would need to be killed for the test, he contends that the procedure is far more humane in that it sacrifices just one animal rather than a dozen or more. Many scientists, however, believe that Muir's test will lose out to that of Dr. Joseph Leighton. The latter is seen as even more humane because it employs a 9-day-old chicken embryo, which has no sense of pain.

Some years ago two researchers devised a method that was meant to reduce the number of animals sacrificed in the LD50 test. Instead of using betwen 40 and 200 animals in their test, they used only 6. Their method consists of first guessing what might be the lethal dose of a substance and injecting it into an animal. They then give additional doses, raising or lowering them, until the amount that caused the animal's death is determined. The test, however, had not replaced the LD50, much to the concern of many scientists who see it as a way of determining a lethal dose with the sacrifice of just a handful of animals.

Useless Experiments
In an attempt to save lives through substitution and reduction, animal advocates are calling for a halt to tests

that are obviously useless. They view as useless the many tests that achieve nothing but a duplication of knowledge learned elsewhere and those that provide information said to be of little or no real value.

The advocates find one area of duplication especially worrisome. Federal law in the United States requires that medical drugs be thoroughly tested even when those same drugs have already been examined and deemed safe in other countries; U.S. regulations do not recognize the evaluations made by other nations. The result is that, in the aim of learning something already known about a drug, countless laboratory animals suffer and die. Immense amounts of money are spent on the tests, and patients in need of the drug are made to wait months or years before it is finally cleared for use.

The history of the drug cromyl sodium (disodium cromoglycate) provides an example of what can happen under current federal law. The drug is considered highly valuable in preventing asthma attacks, having proven itself effective in 80 percent of the patients who have tried it. Tested in Great Britain and found of value, cromyl sodium went on the market there some years ago, but the United States ignored the British findings and subjected it to another decade of testing before clearing it for public use.

Advocates are urging that U.S. regulations be altered so that test results achieved in other nations can be taken into account here. Some government offices involved in setting regulations for the testing of consumer products are responding and beginning to move along this line.

And what of experiments that are said to yield information of little or no general value? Most attacked here are experiments in the field of psychology. To advocates such as writer Patricia Curtis, many such works are not only pointless but also sickeningly cruel.

Psychological Experiments

- In her book *Animal Rights: Stories of People Who Defend the Rights of Animals,* Patricia Curtis focuses much of her outrage on a series of psychological experiments conducted in the early 1970s. These experiments involved taking baby monkeys from their mothers and raising them in boxes without contact with other monkeys or humans. Some of the infants were handed to "mothers" built of wire frames covered by terrycloth. The "mothers" subjected the babies to various types of cruel treatment; one "mother" was electrically heated until it burned the child clinging to it. The young monkeys, Curtis writes, grew up neurotic, severely depressed, and filled with fears. The researchers said that the experiments proved many theories about the fate of human babies who are deprived of their mothers or born to cruel parents.

Curtis is not alone in loathing these experiments; others have heatedly questioned their usefulness. Did the tests actually prove anything of genuine value? Specifically, did they come up with facts that we did not already know from seeing the behavior of unloved and mistreated humans? Did they reveal anything about the effects of being unloved and mistreated that our common sense had not already told us? Were the facts themselves worth the suffering endured by the infant monkeys? And could not the same ends have been achieved through a painless study of human children known to be unloved or abused?

Jeff Diner of the Animal Welfare Institute in Washington, D.,C., is another advocate deeply troubled by such work. In *The Physical and Mental Suffering of Experimental Animals,* a report written in 1979 for the institute, he listed a string of painful and questionable experiments. To mention just one, researchers at the Massachusetts Institute of Technology deliberately blinded hamsters to find out if a type of aggressive behavior could be induced by blinding. Experiments elsewhere have sought to develop a fighting behavior in animals by subjecting them to electric shocks.

The Diner list cannot help but prompt further questions: How did such experiments serve to meet the basic objective of all psychological research—a greater understanding of the mysterious workings of the mind and personality? What of real value was learned by blinding hamsters to see if they would become more aggressive? What of real worth was to be found in subjecting others to electric shocks? In countless minds, the answer is not a thing.

Educational Experimentation
Like much of the psychological research, animal experimentation for educational purposes is an area that animal advocates find useless and repellent. Here, to cite the most obvious example of widespread mistreatment, countless frogs are dissected without anesthetics each year in high school and college classes for the purpose of acquainting the students with some fundamental biological facts.

One California advocate speaks for many when he says,

> It's pathetic. Frogs are being maimed and killed right and left for facts that can be gotten out of any number of textbooks. What's being done is especially pathetic when you stop to think that the great majority of the students aren't ever going to use what they learn and are simply going to forget about it. What's really happening is that we're teaching them more about cruelty than biology. And, what's more, we're damaging many students emotionally. A lot of them aren't going to forget the horror they felt when cutting a frog open.

Equally upsetting are the cruelty and pointlessness seen in so many of the projects invented by students for their classrooms and school science fairs. Patricia Curtis devotes angry paragraphs to some especially cruel and useless projects. She reports on the ninth-grader who won a science-fair prize for smothering several dozen mice over a period of months by placing them in plastic bags, all in the vain—and, as Curtis calls it, outlandish—hope of developing a breed of mice that could breathe through their skins. She goes on to mention another student who, without using an anesthetic, blinded a number of pigeons to see if they could fly without their sight.

The schools themselves and their science teachers are beginning to recognize how repellent and wasteful of animal life are the dissections and science projects. In her book Patricia Curtis reports that there appears to be a growing campaign to prohibit the laboratory use of live animals in U.S. public schools and, further, to ensure that classroom animals are always carefully tended. She lists California, Connecticut, Illinois, Maine, and Pennsylvania as states that have passed laws toward this end. The day may be approaching when dissections and other similar activities are limited to surgical courses in schools of medicine, veterinary medicine, and nursing. There, at the least, the animals are placed under anesthetic and the work can be said to be a necessary part of student training. A national organization of young people was recently formed and is now working to help end classroom dissections. Headquartered in Washington, D.C., the organization is the Student Action Corps for Animals (SACA).

FUNDS FOR THE SEARCH

Several organizations are dedicated to funding and encouraging the search for alternative methods of experimentation. One of the leaders worldwide is the International Association Against Painful Experiments on Animals, which is represented by groups in thirty-nine countries. A major United States organization is the American Fund for Alternatives to Animal Research.

Funding is also coming from a number of companies that test their products with animals, among them Bristol-Meyers and the cosmetic manufacturers Revlon and Estée Lauder. A major example here is Revlon. As the result of pressure exerted by animal advocates, the company is now contributing a percentage of its annual gross income to the Laboratory Animal Research Center at Rockefeller University in New York City. The center is using the funds to find alternatives to the Draize test. In the next chapter, we will see how the animal activists pressured Revlon into providing these funds.

Animal advocates say that these monies are helping not only the lab animals but also the tax-paying public. Much of today's scientific research is paid for by government grants, and animal research involves tremendous costs. On the other hand, the alternative methods of experimentation are proving to be very inexpensive. A case in point is the Ames Test, which requires only forty-eight to seventy-two hours and a few hundred dollars to check the carcinogens in a substance. Similar tests with animals require up to three years and about $150,000 to complete.

ANOTHER SIDE
OF THE STORY

The search for alternative methods of experimentation is just one part of our story. There is, as you will recall from Chapter One, another side. It concerns not the pain and death induced by the experiments themselves but the suffering caused by the careless and inhumane treatment too often shown the animals while they are being housed in the laboratories. Animal advocates are outraged by this treatment and are campaigning to correct matters. What they are doing is so important that it deserves a chapter of its own.

CHAPTER FOUR

ANIMALS FOR SCIENCE: HELPING HANDS

It would be unfair to say that all laboratory animals are carelessly and inhumanely treated while awaiting, undergoing, and then recovering from experiments; some laboratories provide attentive and sympathetic care. But a growing number of news reports in the 1980s have left no doubt that a great many lab animals do suffer terrible abuse.

The reports speak of animals housed in cages and kennels that are never—or only rarely—cleaned of fecal matter and unused food. They speak of animals that are not given pain killers between experiments, of animals with surgical incisions and sores left unattended, and of animals that do not even receive adequate amounts of water and food.

The information on which these reports are based has often come from sensitive researchers who have been appalled at what they have seen. In other cases the information has been obtained by advocate groups that have investigated laboratories or, as we will soon see, broken into them at night.

There are also reports of researchers who actually

torment and torture the animals under their care. While working undercover as a lab assistant, one advocate not only saw researchers tease the animals and shake their cages but also watched a researcher stick a pair of pliers between an animal's teeth while the creature was held in a restraining device. The lab assistant later became the cofounder of People for the Ethical Treatment of Animals, one of the most influential animal rights groups in the United States today.

Caring people everywhere—including the many researchers who are humiliated by the cruel torments inflicted by some of their colleagues—have been outraged by the reports. Individually and in groups, they have taken action. They are working to better the living conditions endured by the animals and, of course, to end the painful experimentation itself. Working along two fronts, they are

Striving to alert the public to the suffering so that there will be a growing sympathy for the animals and, as a result, a growing demand that their rights be respected and their suffering ended.

Seeking changes in the law to ensure greater protections for the animals.

HELPING HANDS:
ALERTING THE PUBLIC

As you know, national and international organizations dedicated to animal welfare have existed for a long while, with some dating back to the nineteenth century. Most are concerned not only with the treatment shown laboratory animals but also with the well-being of all animals. Included among these many organizations are such U.S. groups as the National Antivivisection Society, the American Humane Association, the Humane Society of the United States, and the American Society for the Prevention of Cruelty to Animals. Working to the north is the Canadian Federation of Humane Societies.

Recent years have seen new groups join these long-time organizations and come to the aid of animals. One of the newcomers is Mobilization for Animals (MFA), which is headquartered in Washington, D.C. A coalition of thirty-one protective organizations, MFA devotes much time to testifying at state and federal legislative hearings on the adoption of laws against the use of animals in research. Another is the International Primate Protection League. The league works from its South Carolina base to safeguard nonhuman primates in laboratories as well as zoos and the wilds. Still another group is the Animal Welfare Institute The Institute, with its main office located in Washington, D.C., seeks humane treatment for many types of animals, especially those used in medicine and research. (These are just three of the many groups at work today. A more complete list of U.S. animal protection organizations and their addresses is to be found at the end of this book.)

All the above groups and many of their fellow organizations are seeking to help lab animals through peaceful means. Virtually all of them publish materials—from newspapers and magazines to booklets and pamphlets—that point out the suffering endured in the laboratories and the possible steps for alleviating or ending it. Some distribute audiovisual and other educational materials. Some send representatives to speak at civic, school, and club meetings. Some, as MFA, work with local, state, and federal leaders to develop protective laws.

MILITANT HANDS

The 1980s, however, have seen the formation of groups whose means of alerting the public to the animal problem is anything but peaceful. Bearing such names as the Urban Guerrillas, the Band of Mercy, and the Animal Liberation Front, these militant groups have sought to get their message across to the public by means of street demonstrations and raids on research facilities. These raids have seen the Band of Mercy free—or, as the group said, "liberate"—some forty rabbits from a laboratory on the University of Maryland campus. The Urban Guerrillas have freed cats from research work being done at the University of California at Berkeley.

The best known of the militant groups is the Animal Liberation Front (ALF). Of undetermined size because its membership is kept secret, it has in recent years raided laboratories in the United States, Great Britain, and elsewhere, damaging equipment and often freeing the laboratory animals. It made headlines in December 1984, when a band of raiders was sent into the City of Hope National Medical Center at Duarte in Southern California and took away 115 animals said to be living in terrible conditions. The ALF's most publicized raid, however, came earlier that year. It was directed against the Head Injury Clinical Research Center in Philadelphia, Pennsylvania. The Head Injury Center's work is funded by federal money that is placed with the National Institutes of Health (NIH) and then passed on to research facilities in the form of grants.

Target: The Head Injury
Clinical Research Center
Working in laboratories on the campus of the University of Pennsylvania, the Head Injury Clinical Research Center has spent thirteen years studying various head injuries in the hope of finding improved methods of treating the victims of automobile accidents. Between $11 million and $13 million in NIH grants have been spent on the work and its experiments. Estimates hold that about eighty primates—monkeys, baboons, and

chimpanzees—have been subjected to the experiments.

The ALF raiders broke into the laboratories just before dawn on May 28, 1984. They smashed test equipment and poured acid into computers, with University of Pennsylvania sources stating that about $40,000 in damage was done. The raiders then stole thirty-two videotapes (some press reports say thirty-three) made of the center's work over the past six years. The tapes added up to more than sixty hours' worth of viewing.

The ALF passed the tapes along to the activist group People for the Ethical Treatment of Animals (PETA), an 80,000-member organization seeking legislation to protect animals of all types. PETA edited the tapes down to a thirty-minute presentation that was shown on television stations in various parts of the country. It was made available for viewing to various groups and individuals, including members of the U.S. Congress. The reaction of all the viewers was a combination of shock and outrage. They found the experiments shown brutal, even though the center claimed that the test animals had been anesthetized beforehand. Viewers spoke of watching animals have their necks broken. Reporter William Robbin, in a June 1984 edition of *The New York Times*, wrote of one sequence in which a struggling monkey was strapped to a table while its head was locked in a steel cylinder attached to a pneumatic machine. A piston in the machine then suddenly drove the cylinder upward and sent the monkey's head sharply through a 60-degree arc. The machine was intended to simulate neck and head action in a car crash.

Other viewers claimed that the test animals were housed in unsanitary conditions. Perhaps most troubling was the fact that the tape showed some researchers treating the animals in a callous manner, often poking fun at them or smoking during surgical procedures. In

September 1984 the newspaper *Whole Earth Times* reported that one researcher giggled while working on an animal, saying, "It's a good thing the antivivisectionists will never see this." Viewer James Kilpatrick, a syndicated columnist who says he is *not* an antivivisectionist, found the tapes "appalling" and recalled the laboratory assistant who waved a dazed chimpanzee's limp arms as if they were those of a "rag doll" and joked about "the trainer" who had taught the animal to do "these tricks." There was laughter off-screen. William Robbin, in his *New York Times* report, mentioned the researcher who called his animal subject a "sucker" while looking for brain damage.

Despite the taped evidence of cruelty, the University of Pennsylvania and the National Institutes of Health defended the center. They called it one of the world's finest and best-equipped laboratories and described its research into what happens to the brain at the moment of an accident as vital to the improved treatment of head injuries. One university official said that the center's experiments were on the threshold of major advances in treatment. He went on to say that primates were the only useful subjects for the experiments. And, as was mentioned earlier, the claim was made that, though the tape showed moving animals, they were all anesthetized during experimentation. Many physicians, on viewing the tapes, disputed this claim.

The defense put up by the center came to nothing. Many of the members of Congress who saw the ALF

A primate in restraining gear undergoing a laboraory test to determine the extent of brain damage in head injuries

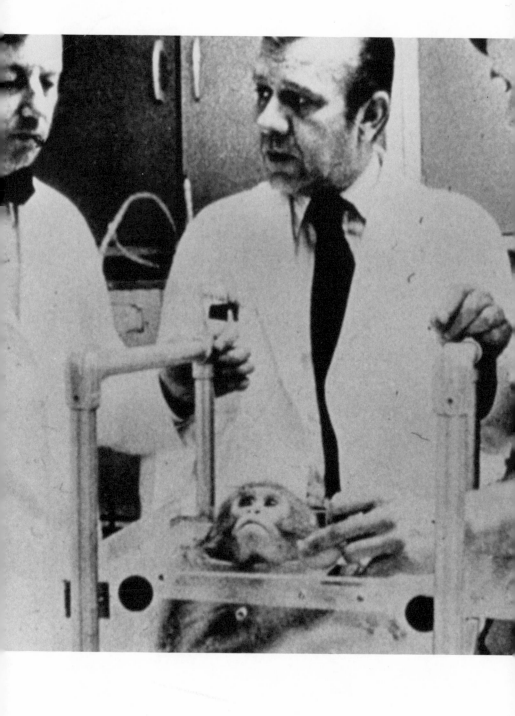

tape immediately wrote to Margaret Heckler, who was the U.S. Secretary of Health and Human Services at the time. (As Secretary, Mrs. Heckler held overall responsibility for U.S. medical and scientific funding.) They condemned the clinic and demanded that NIH grants to it be halted immediately. Further pressure on Mrs. Heckler came from PETA. Founded in 1980, People for the Ethical Treatment of Animals is widely regarded as America's most activist animal organization. It acts as spokesman for the ALF and cooperates in publicizing the messages of the country's many advocate groups, regardless of their type. As a result of all the pressure, the NIH established a committee to investigate the center and its procedures.

In July 1985 some 100 activists, claiming that the committee investigation was moving too slowly, staged a sit-in at NIH headquarters in Bethesda, Maryland. On the fourth day of the sit-in, Mrs. Heckler stepped in. She had aides view the tape and, after hearing their comments, ordered the NIH to suspend its funding of the center for the time being. She also called for a preliminary report from the committee and a further investigation of the center. When issued, the report held that there had been a "material failure" by the center "to comply with public health policy for the care and use of laboratory animals."

In October 1985 Mrs. Heckler said that the center's funds were to be suspended indefinitely. The suspension remains in effect today. Animal rights activists look on this decision as one of their great victories—perhaps their greatest—to date.

White-coated researchers
experiment on a monkey.

Public Opinion: Condemnation

Public opinion is sharply divided over the activities of the ALF and other militant groups. Some people condemn the groups; others applaud them.

The groups are condemned on several counts. They are accused of taking the law into their own hands and thus promoting lawlessness as a means of solving problems; this weakens the understanding that civilized actions are necessary for the survival of any society. Some critics say that ALF members depend on violence to attain their goals and are no better than terrorist bands. Others say that they destroy property, jeopardize valuable work, and frighten people; that they damage the fabric of the entire society; and that they damage the animal rights movement by outraging great segments of the public and giving the mistaken impression that the entire movement is as "crackpot" as they.

There is also the charge that the ALF often employs tactics that are foolish and pointless, as was witnessed in a recent incident on the University of California campus at Davis just outside the state capital in which the ALF placed fake bombs on the front porches of two directors of the school's center for primate research. In other instances the homes of researchers in the United States and Britain have been splattered with paint.

For many people, the group's most outrageous and pointless action was that taken in Great Britain during November 1984. On a Saturday morning a woman who identified herself only as Vivien called a London newspaper and said that the ALF had injected rat poison into Mars candy bars and had placed them on store shelves in various parts of the country. The action was intended, she said, to cut into the profits of the manufacturer, Mars U.K., Ltd., and to make the public aware of the company's animal research activities. The firm sponsors research with monkeys to study the dental effects of a sugar diet. The ALF accused the company of cruelly treating the monkeys, force-feeding them sugar products, and subjecting them to painful dental experiments.

Vivien's call triggered a nationwide hunt for the poisoned candy bars. Days later the police announced that some twenty bars had been found with poison warnings slipped into their wrappers; in some six cities bars were discovered with needlelike punctures in their wrappers. Tests showed that the bars were not tainted and there was no word of anyone being made ill by a Mars bar, but there were numerous reports of frightened parents rushing their children to the hospital on learning that the youngsters had eaten the candy.

Then an ALF spokesman announced that the poison scare had been a hoax. The British government quickly and angrily denounced the group, saying that it had terrorized the 3 million Britons who daily buy Mars candy and had needlessly damaged the firm's reputation. A representative of the Royal Society for the Protection of Cruelty to Animals added his voice to the anger. He said that the hoax had in no way eased "the plight of the animals which the extremist group claim to care about." A Mars executive claimed that the research project monkeys are neither cruelly treated nor force-fed the company's candy. He claimed that the animals simply receive Mars bars as part of their regular diet. Animal activists claim that the Mars firm has now turned to less painful dental experiments.

Public Opinion: Applause
Applause for the militant groups is just as great as the criticism. Their supporters contend that extremist action is necessary, understandable, and successful. The feeling is that such action is needed because peaceful efforts are too slow-moving and have achieved too few solid results over the past years. It is understandable because the militants have been driven to their angry measures

by the continuing animal suffering, and that it is successful is made clear by the Head Injury Center victory. Furthermore, advocates argue that many animal cruelties would have remained unknown to the public had not activist raiders entered labs such as the Head Injury Center and let the world see and hear what they had found.

In addition to the Head Injury Center, supporters of the extremist action can point to another recent victory, one involving the Revlon cosmetics firm. You will recall from Chapter Three that Revlon is now funding a new animal research program at Rockefeller University that hopes to find alternatives to the notorious Draize test. According to an article written by William Severini Kowinski for a 1984 issue of *The Daily News Magazine,* Revlon was pressured into the funding by militant action.

The central figure in Kowinski's article is Henry Spira, a man in his late fifties and a former seaman and high school teacher. Kowinski writes that Spira worked on behalf of animals rights for ten years and then decided to move against the Draize test. Spira visited a high-ranking Revlon executive and proposed that the firm contribute 0.01 percent of its gross annual income—or about $240,000—to finding a Draize replacement. The visit came to nothing, with Revlon saying that it was conducting its own research. Quickly, demonstrators appeared at the company's headquarters in New York City, some dressed in bunny suits and most carrying placards protesting Revlon's use of the Draize test. The campaign was furthered by a number of ads placed in *The New York Times* by the activists. The ads triggered a widespread sympathetic outcry for the animals. In what Kowinski calls "a remarkably short time," Revlon began its funding of the new research program at Rockefeller University.

HELPING HANDS: CHANGES

The militant groups are generally correct in saying that peaceful efforts are slow-moving. Such has usually been the case in every area of life. But they are dead wrong to think that peaceful efforts do not produce meaningful results. The peaceful side of the animal rights movement is now bringing about definite changes in the treatment of laboratory animals before, during, and after experimentation. And, as the public becomes increasingly aware of what is happening in the world's laboratories, the changes are happening with greater frequency.

We have already spoken of some of these changes. There is, of course, the all-important search for alternative methods of experimentation and the wise movement away from using animals for school experimentation and science fair projects.

Additionally, the manner in which laboratories house and tend their animals is coming under closer scrutiny. For example, in 1985 the U.S. Public Health Service (PHS) revised its policy concerning lab animals. Like the National Institutes of Health, the PHS provides government funds for research projects, and it has always maintained a policy calling for humane treatment by the labs receiving its funds. The new revision strengthens that policy. It requires that institutions seeking PHS money provide strong justification for the use of animals in planned experiments. It also calls for the institutions to maintain a high standard of animal care and furnish the federal government with detailed information on all aspects of that care—from the animal quarters themselves to the qualifications of the staff assigned to tend the animals. Failure of a research project to meet these demands can result in the loss of its PHS funding.

On their own, a number of institutions are working

to improve their lab facilities. One of them—California's Stanford University—opened a new research center in mid-1985. Costing $11 million, the 30,000-square-foot (2,790 sq m) installation is being called one of the nation's most modern and best-equipped animal research facilities. It includes surgical suites and such animal accommodations as intensive care units, stainless steel cages, a system of fans and ventilators able to change the air more than twenty times a minute, and special rooms that keep test subjects infected with dangerous diseases well away from the rest of the animal population.

Stanford officials say that the facility was built for greater lab efficiency and to end the animal advocate criticism that the university could not provide humane living conditions for its animals. Many advocates, however, are unhappy with the installation: They contend that, no matter how modern it may be, it is still the scene of animal suffering and death.

HELPING HANDS:
IMPROVING ANIMAL LAWS

Of especially great importance are the efforts now underway to replace the current protective laws governing lab animals. These efforts do not seek to ban animal experimentation, for a ban, as we saw earlier, is considered impractical by most animal advocates because the public would object to the resultant delay in research aimed at ending the world's most dreaded diseases. Rather, the hope is to pass laws that will better the lot of the test subjects in various ways. These laws are being sought at both the state and federal levels.

At the State Level
At the time of this writing, bills seeking to protect lab animals have been introduced for consideration by the

legislatures of some twenty-one states. Some of the bills, such as one under discussion in Arizona, would protect stray pets and homeless animals from experimentation. Hitherto, pounds have often disposed of these animals by selling them to dealerships that, in turn, peddle them to laboratories.

Other state bills are calling for a reduction in the number of animals assigned to experimentation. For example, a bill being considered in Massachusetts would require the number of test animals used by an institution to be reduced by 5 percent each year. The aim here is to encourage the development of alternative methods of experimentation.

Still other state bills are aimed at improving the living conditions of laboratory animals. Again Massachusetts must be mentioned; before its legislators is a proposed law that would give humane societies the power to make unannounced inspections of any installation housing animals for commercial, educational, or scientific purposes.

At the Federal Level

Since 1966 a federal law—the Animal Welfare Act—has sought to protect laboratory animals from inhumane treatment and housing. Congress passed the act after learning of the terrible living conditions found in many labs and animal dealerships. The act was expanded in 1970 and again in 1978 to safeguard animals in zoos, circuses, pet stores, and other similar facilities.

Though considered better than no law at all, the act is viewed as extremely weak by most advocates. They consider it an inadequate safety measure for two reasons: First, its protection is not extended to all animals; specifically mentioned for protection are dogs, cats, primates, rabbits, and hamsters, but omitted are rats and mice—the little creatures that make up 70 percent of all U.S. lab animals. Second, the act calls for the use of anesthetics and pain killers but does not require them if the researchers feel that the observation of pain is necessary to the judging of an experiment. Thus the act can be easily sidestepped, as is now often being done with the Draize test. Many researchers, you will recall, are resisting the growing use of anesthetics in the Draize test because pain killers may alter such factors as blinking.

As this book is being written, two members of the U.S. Congress are attempting to strengthen the Animal Welfare Act: Senator Robert Dole (Republican, Kansas) and Representative George E. Brown (Democrat, California) have introduced identical bills for congressional consideration and passage. Both bills call for six improvements in the act and require that

Careful pre- and postsurgical care be given to all test animals.

Pain-relieving drugs be given to minimize suffering.

Paralytic drugs (now used to keep animals from crying out) be prohibited unless anesthetics are also given.

The repeated use of the same animal for painful experiments be avoided.

The fine for violating the Animal Welfare Act be set at $2,500 (the present fine is $1,000).

The search for alternative methods of experimentation be continued.

The twin bills have won much approval among animal advocates, some scientists, and many national legislators. With a total ban on the use of laboratory animals being regarded as unacceptable to the public, the bills are seen as a practical solution to a knotty problem.

Striking a balance between the needs of science and those of the test subjects, they allow animal research to continue while providing increased protection for the animals. The bills are being backed by many animal advocate groups, among them the Associated Humane Societies. Support is also coming from such scientific groups as the American Institute of Biological Sciences, an organization representing thirty biological societies.

But the support is not universal. The bills are opposed by some animal advocates—especially those of a militant bent—on the grounds that they are weak and do little to eradicate animal research. The bills are also opposed by the Association of Biomedical Research, a trade group representing the suppliers of animals to research labs.

In October 1985, the Dole measure became part of a major farm bill being considered by the U.S. Senate. The bill is under senate study as this book is being written and may be enacted into law in late 1985 or early 1986. Because of the Dole measure's placement in the farm bill, the Brown measure has faded from congressional attention. However, since both measures are identical, the lab animals will benefit just as much from the Dole bill alone.

And so only time will tell whether the Dole measure will be enacted and bring relief to countless lab animals, and only time will tell whether the current advances in the search for alternative methods of experimentation will eventually see all animals set free. But, whatever the outcome, it can be said that major steps are being taken today in these happy directions.

CHAPTER FIVE

ANIMALS FOR COMMERCE: FACTORY FARMING

In their age-old role of servants to humans, animals have done far more than pull our wagons, endure scientific experimentation, and give us companionship as pets. They have also provided us with many products for our consumption, products that range from those we feel are necessary for survival to those that simply please our fancies—everything from food to fur coats and stylish footwear.

The animals provide us with these commercial products today at a cost they have always borne at human hands, the cost of pain and death. It is a cost that, worldwide, takes *billions* of animal lives yearly. To see it at close hand, we will now look at two ways in which those lives are being sacrificed for commerce. In this chapter we will talk about the agricultural system called factory farming. The trapping of animals for their pelts will be the subject of Chapter Six.

FACTORY FARMING

The family farm that produces meat, poultry, eggs, milk, and vegetables for the market is fast disappearing from the scene in the world's advanced countries, Great Britain and the United States among them. It is being replaced by large companies that, in order to meet the consumer demands of growing populations at home and abroad, are replacing the old farm ways with modern production methods that can supply greater quantities of food far more quickly.

Animal advocates, while admitting that hunger in various parts of the globe makes any improvement in the world's food supply desirable, look on these modern methods with horror. They are efficient methods, yes, but they are also heartlessly brutal. They do not treat the animals as living creatures with needs dictated by their natures. No longer are chickens permitted to scamper about and scratch the ground as they once did in the barnyard. No longer are pigs allowed to cool their skins with contented rolls in a muddy pen. No longer are cattle, cows, and sheep free to graze in open fields. Rather, they are jammed together in spaces too small for movement, fed mechanically, shown no concern, and then just as mechanically slaughtered.

In all, the natures, welfare, and comfort of the animals are totally ignored for the sake of production methods that seek the greatest profit possible at the least possible cost in housing and care. These methods are known in agriculture as "intensive livestock husbandry" and "total confinement." Animal advocates greet the two terms with contempt and brand them as pleasant disguises for brutality. The advocates refer angrily to the system as "factory farming."

In the United States, as elsewhere, factory farming has become a major commercial enterprise that is threatening the family farm with extinction. About 80 percent of all U.S. agricultural products, animal and nonanimal alike, are factory farmed. As for the animals themselves, 70 percent of all the mammals and 98 percent of all the poultry (chickens, turkeys, ducks, geese, ducks, and guinea fowl) that reach American tables come from factory farms. Approximately 150 million mammals and more than 3 billion poultry animals are killed annually for the nation's restaurants and homes—far outdistancing the number of laboratory animals sacrificed worldwide each year.

Just how brutal is factory farming? To see, we need only look at what is done to one animal—the chicken. Its fate more than aptly illustrates what is happening to all food animals.

CHICKEN FARMING

Of all poultry animals, chickens are the ones most in demand for food. As is true on the small farm, they are raised for two purposes in factory farming: to lay eggs and to be eaten. The chickens that produce eggs are known in the business as "layers," and those to be eaten as "broilers."

Layer Chickens
The term *total confinement* truly applies to the layers. They spend their lives in wire-mesh cages that usually measure 18 to 20 square inches (46 to 51 sq cm). The cages are mounted in tiers three or more stories high in giant shedlike buildings called layer houses. Usually three to five chickens are jammed together in one cage. As many as 90,000 layers can be found in a single layer house.

Crowded as they are, the chickens have no space in which to move and are forced into an agonizing immobility that is completely alien to their natures. Furthermore, there are no perches on which they can rest and, making matters even worse, the floors are slanted so that the lain eggs can roll out of the cages, tumbling through an opening and then dropping onto a conveyor belt that carries them off to be processed and crated.

Machinery surrounds the cages. Not only is there

the conveyor belt for carrying the eggs away, but also there is one that passes by with food and water. The chicken droppings fall through the wire-mesh floors onto wide strips of sheet metal on the roofs of the cages beneath. The waste is then swept to a nearby pit by means of a mechanical scraper. Another scraper transfers the waste to an outside dump when the pit is full. Rarely, if ever, does a comforting human touch replace the machinery for even a moment.

These stressful conditions quickly take their toll. The animals express their anger and frustration by clawing and pecking at each other. Exhaustion is seen as many chickens lose their color, develop brittle bones, and find themselves unable to stand. All are symptoms of a disorder known as cage layer fatigue, a condition rarely, if ever, found in chickens raised on traditional farms and given the chance to exercise by running about the barnyard. The factory farmers attempt to reduce the stress and maintain egg production by keeping the layerhouse lights turned low most of the time. For all but a few hours each day, the chickens live in semidarkness, cheated of even the impression of sunlight.

Layer chickens can be expected to live for fifteen to twenty years on a family farm. The stresses imposed by the factory farm reduces their life span to about one year. As that year goes by, the tired and upset layers produce fewer and fewer eggs. Some factory farmers "force-molt" their hens in an effort to renew egg production. This is done by suddenly stopping their food and water and cutting back on the few hours of light allowed the birds daily. The resultant shock kills some of the birds but prompts others to increase their laying. The measure works for a time, but soon the egg production falls off again. When the hens can no longer lay enough eggs to merit their keep, they are sold to soup and pet food manufacturers.

For many of the birds, death comes soon after birth.

Chicks are born at hatcheries and shipped a few weeks later to the layer farms. On emerging from their shells, the newborn are sent along conveyor belts manned by workers who separate them according to sex at the rate of 2,000 an hour. The hens are set aside for shipment. The males are killed, usually by being stuffed into plastic bags until suffocation results.

Broiler Chickens

Life is no better for the broiler chickens. Although there is presently a trend toward housing them in cages, most broilers spend their lives crowded together on the floors of great sheds. Some sheds can house as many as 90,000 birds at a time. The animals are fattened over a period of eight to ten weeks before being slaughtered.

In common with the layer hens, the broilers soon show their anger and exhaustion. Fighting is common, a problem that the farmers dislike because injuries can damage the look and quality of the meat that is soon to be sold. The problem is solved by feeding the chickens tranquilizing chemicals and subjecting them to two minor but painful surgical procedures, toe clipping and debeaking. Both are done with a hot-knife machine, with toe-clipping slicing away the claws and debeaking cutting off about half of the upper and lower beaks. Usually performed in haste so that their costs can be kept low, the operations are often done carelessly and the birds are left with torn feet, damaged mouth tissue, and burned or cut tongues.

In the modern factory farm, fowl spend their short lives crowded into great sheds. Inset: the chicken on the left has been debeaked, but the lower beak has grown back.

The brutality of these procedures, however, pales when compared to that of the system used to kill the birds for marketing. To begin, workers called catchers enter the shed at night, when the birds are less restless. The catchers herd them into one corner, snatch them up, and shove them into crates for shipment to the processing plant, or—bluntly—the slaughterhouse. On arrival there, workers in a "hanging crew" take over. They unpack the animals and attach them by both feet to a conveyor belt. Hanging from the belt and screaming and twisting in fright until the blood rushing to their heads quiets them, the chickens travel to a worker who stuns them with an electric shock to the head and neck. This is done in keeping with the federal government's 1958 Humane Slaughter Act, which, as you will recall, requires that all food animals be spared pain by stunning before being killed. Also, unless stunned, the birds might continue to flap about and damage their meat.

After stunning, the conveyor moves the birds to an automatic slaughter machine. The machine first catches the heads in a channel-like holder. The holder keeps the heads motionless and in place as the conveyor continues its trip through the machine to a radial saw for decapitation. From there the conveyor leads to an area where the birds are allowed to bleed dry, after which they are sent into vats of scalding water for cleaning and defeathering.

The grisly work continues as the chickens are eviscerated (the internal organs removed), dismembered, and packaged. A processing plant can do all its work at the rate of 6,000 animals per hour.

OTHER ANIMALS

Although the commercial rearing and processing of chickens provides a memorable example of what goes on in the factory farming system, some mention of the plight of their fellow creatures will help round out the picture. The following are some examples of the sufferings of the other animals destined to provide us with food.

Dairy and Beef Cattle

Statistics show that about half the dairy cows in the United States are factory farmed. They spend much of their time in stalls within giant barns and are usually milked by means of automatic machines. As many as 80 to over 120 cows can be found in a single barn. On some factory farms the cows are allowed to move about within or just outside the barn; on others they must remain in their stalls at all times, sometimes held in place by chain leashes attached to the walls.

There is little doubt that the stall system with its milking machinery helps to keep down the price paid by the consumer for dairy products. This is because the costs of traditional dairy farming—the costs of the land for grazing and the expense of employing human milkers—have grown greater in recent years. They are costs that would have to be passed on to the consumer by any farmer who hopes to stay in business.

But this is an economy won through discomfort for the animals. For one, the cows are forced to stand on slatted floors so that their waste matter will drop through the openings between the slats. An even greater economy is achieved here because not as many workers are now needed to clean the stalls. But the floors still catch some of the manure and become slippery, causing the cows to stumble. Animal hooves sometimes become caught in the openings and are bruised or otherwise harmed.

For another, the cows are made to breed continually. Like other mammals, they give milk only at the time their young are born. Their milking time lasts about ten months before stopping. To secure new milk quickly, the farmers breed the cows again as soon as possible after they've given birth. Breeding is usually done through artificial insemination, the placing of male semen in the female by artificial means.

Beef cattle, though raised not for milking but for marketing as food, live much as do the dairy cows. They too are housed for months in stalls with slatted floors; they too sustain injuries when they slip or catch their hooves in the openings between the slats (the farmers do not see these mishaps as a problem because the animals will be slaughtered before the injuries develop into conditions that will spread and damage the meat). The cattle too are usually not allowed to breed naturally but are subjected to artificial insemination. And, as are the cows, they are fed grain mixtures to which hormones are added. Such feed helps increase the dairy cow's milk production and fattens the beef cattle for slaughter.

Veal Calves
The milk that a cow produces is, of course, meant for her newborn calf, but most calves today are not given the benefit of that milk because it is a product meant for sale. When calves are a day or so old, they are separated from their mothers, with some then being nutured on grains and the such until they themselves are ready for breeding and milking. At the time of the separation, the calves are divided according to sex and quality. The males and those females judged to be of poor quality are useless to the dairy farmer and are sold to factory farms that will raise them for marketing as veal.

Because veal is obtained from young cows, the calves are allowed to survive for only thirteen to fifteen weeks before being slaughtered. They spend that time standing in individual stalls that are hardly wider and longer than their bodies. They are fed only an artificial milk with a high fat content and no iron. This pushes the calves' weight up to a very profitable 300 to 350 pounds (136 to 159 kg) and, at the same time, induces anemia, a condition that gives their meat the pale pink color (the farmers refer to it as "white") so desired by veal lovers.

Not even hay is placed in the stalls to provide a bit of comfort should the calves lie down, for hay contains iron. In their instinctive search for iron, the calves often gnaw at their stall bars. The lack of this vital mineral element kills about 10 percent of the calves. The rest are fed various antibiotics to protect against the diseases that imprisonment and poor diet can bring.

Pork Animals

The factory farming methods that prepare pork for market usually involve several steps. First, there is the breeding of sows to produce the piglets that will eventually find their way to our dinner tables. Once bred, a sow spends about 100 days in a stall while gestation takes place; then, when ready to give birth, she is transferred to a farrowing stall. This stall, which has a concrete floor, is only slightly larger than the sow herself, usually measuring about 2 by 6 feet (0.6 x 1.83 m). This size is chosen because the farmers do not want the sow to roll about during and after birth and crush any of her valuable piglets. To guard further against movement, a farmer will sometimes tie the sow to the floor.

Under normal conditions newly born piglets suckle the mother for two months or more; in factory farming, however, it is economically vital to breed the sow again quickly so that she can produce new young for the market. Consequently, she is taken from her piglets in anywhere from two days to one week or so and returned to the breeding area. The piglets are transferred to individual pens and fed automatically until they are big enough for a shift to the "finishing pens," the cramped stalls in which they will stay until the time comes for their slaughter.

The finishing pens measure about 10 by 12 feet (3.05 x 3.66 m) and can hold a dozen or more pigs at a time. The floors—made of metal, concrete, or plastic—are slatted for the usual purpose of allowing the animals' excrement to fall through to the ground beneath. The animals are packed together so tightly that, like the chickens, they eventually vent their anger and frustration in fighting. They snap at one another and at the pen bars. There was a time when such fighting resulted in the pigs biting one another's tails off, but the factory farmers now avoid this problem by amputating the tails before the piglets go to the pens.

A pig's normal life span ranges from ten to twelve years; in factory farming the animals are allowed to survive for four to six months before being slaughtered.

WHAT CAN BE DONE
ABOUT THE SUFFERING?

This question can best be answered by first describing what is already being done to help factory-farmed animals. Only a few steps have been taken on their behalf. For one, several countries—notably Denmark, Great Britain, Sweden, and West Germany—have enacted laws aimed at more humane confinement practices. A good example of such protective legislation is to be seen in Great Britain, where in 1981 a government committee investigated factory farming and immediately established a set of new standards for the system to follow. These standards require that (1) straw bedding be provided for pigs, and solid food for cattle, (2) pigs and sows not be raised in solitary confinement or in darkness, and (3) calves be placed in pens large enough to enable them to turn around and lie down.

For another, the United States still has its Humane Slaughter Act of 1958 on the books, and federal legislators have been discussing ways in which the animal suffering might be further reduced. For yet another, an Arizona meat company has adopted a more humane system of slaughter that could be easily used throughout the industry. Called the Stairway to Heaven, this method involves sending cattle to their death to the accompaniment of soothing recorded music. Then, on being hoisted into a body-length restrainer, the animals are immediately rendered unconscious with a stunner device. The Arizona firm claims that the system spares the animals panic and pain.

These, however, are just about the only steps that have been taken to date. In the eyes of all animal advocates, they are too few, and, in the eyes of many, they are useless for two reasons. First, the laws established by Great Britain and a few other countries, though well intentioned in their effort to ensure more housing space and a better diet, still allow the animals to be penned in circumstances contrary to their needs and natures. Second, not one of the above measures prohibits the wholesale slaughter of the animals.

The steps have been so few because it is difficult, even close to impossible, to make changes in the law that would significantly better the lot of the animals and significantly reduce the number today being sacrificed. The factory farmer would balk at changes for the better—such as greater freedom for each animal—because they would entail greater production costs; the consumer, likewise, would complain because those increased production costs would lead to higher prices at the market.

As for curbing the animal slaughter, you can assuredly count on widespread public resistance to any such idea. The people of the world's meat-eating countries are accustomed to a flesh diet, like it, and believe that the protein yielded by meat is necessary for good health. They currently would not stand still for measures that would put a ceiling on the number of animals killed annually or that would seek to outlaw altogether the slaughtering of animals for food.

So what can be done to help the victims of factory farming? Animal advocates feel that individual action can do much here. They offer a number of suggestions that you yourself can put to effective use. The following suggestions, if enough people followed them, could well lead to healthy changes in factory farming practices and to tougher laws governing its activities:

Learn about the many organizations working on behalf of the animals. Add your voice to theirs by joining one or more of their number. (A representative list of these organizations can be found at the end of this book.)

Make every attempt not to buy factory farm products. Rather, seek out those markets (or farms if you live in or near a rural area) that feature meat and poultry products coming from the traditional farm. You will hit the factory farmers where it hurts most—in their pocketbooks—and help keep the fast-disappearing traditional farm from vanishing altogether.

Reduce or even eliminate your consumption of meat. Today's meat eaters, because of their sometimes insatiable appetites and because of factory farming's tremendous output, are devouring more flesh than ever before. This is especially true in the United States, where the average person eats more than 200 pounds (90 kg) of red meat and poultry per year. You can easily reduce your consumption by cutting back from a meat dish daily to one every three days or even one a week. Your health will not suffer if you replace the meat dishes with other high-protein foods—and you will find that there are many of them just waiting for your attention.

Take a serious look at vegetarianism if you think you would like to eliminate flesh from your diet altogether. Again, you will find plenty of other protein-rich foods at hand. You will also find that the shape and size of our jaws, teeth, and mouths indicate that we were not intended to eat meat in the first place—that we are herbivorous rather than carnivorous animals. And, as a vegetarian, you will also be helping to spare an animal that, though not mentioned thus far, is one of the major sharers of our planet: the fish.

Animal suffering is not the only problem that the advocates and others see in factory farming. There is widespread fear that the system poses terrible dangers for the public's health.

There is certainly nothing healthful about the filth that meat processing has produced in some areas. According to writer Ron Litton, a recent study of the meat-packing industry in Omaha, Nebraska, revealed that the city's packers daily deposited 100,000 pounds (45,000 kg) of grease, intestinal waste, carcass dressing, and fecal matter into the sewers. This pollution was then emptied into the Missouri River.

Furthermore, there is the growing outcry that the meat being produced by animals frustrated and angry by their confinement is of poor quality compared to the meat that once came from the traditional farm.

Finally, there is an increasing amount of evidence to suggest that the very eating of meat holds some terrible dangers for humans. Statistics, for example, show that the death rate from heart disease is high in countries such as Australia, Canada, and the United States, where meat consumption is high. The death rate is lowest in nations such as Japan and Italy, where meat consumption is low. Many scientists are warning us about the drugs, hormones, and antibiotics fed to the animals and about the pesticides used to ward off disease in the pens and stalls. These substances are passed on to us in the meat and constitute a threat because certain of their number have been found to be potential carcinogens. The same goes for the chemicals in which some meat is dipped to give it a more attractive color. As Dr. John W. Berg wrote in a 1973 issue of *The Wall Street Journal* newspaper, there is substantial evidence to show that the eating of beef is connected with the incidence of bowel cancer.

In all, the situation is one of vast irony. On the one hand, countless laboratory animals are being sacrificed in today's quest to rid the world of its most dreaded diseases; on the other, countless animals are being killed to give us meats that—because of the ways in which they are produced and because the meats themselves may be dangerous—loom as harmful and even fatal to our health. It is a situation that concerned people everywhere feel must, in one way or another, be corrected as soon as possible.

CHAPTER SIX

ANIMALS FOR COMMERCE: THE CLUBBED AND TRAPPED

This chapter brings us to the animals that are hunted and trapped commercially so that their pelts can be used to make certain types of clothing. Sacrificed worldwide each year are land, freshwater, and sea animals that include the beaver, bobcat, coyote, fox, mink, muskrat, otter, rabbit, raccoon, sable, seal, and woodchuck.

No one knows exactly how many animals die annually throughout the world for the very profitable fur business, but a statistic from just one area serves as an indication: Canadian and American fur trappers alone take the lives of at least 13 million animals a year.

COMMERCIAL HUNTING AND TRAPPING

In earlier days the people of the world hunted and trapped fur-bearing animals out of necessity, for both food and clothing. Today, in all but a few areas of the globe, the food yielded by the fur bearers is disliked and has been replaced by tastier fare. And today, again in all but a very few places, the need to use furs for clothing has disappeared. Fur has been replaced by various other materials, all providing just as much warmth for a price that is usually much lower. Even the Eskimos of the Arctic regions are turning more and more to parkas as substitutes for their traditional fur apparel.

Today's furs do little else but give us expensive or expensive-looking coats, jackets, stoles, hats, and gloves. Many of these items, such as sable coats, are genuinely costly and can carry price tags of several thousands of dollars each. Others, such as jackets made of rabbit fur, are inexpensive and can often be had for under one hundred dollars. Most fur items, especially coats, are worn as signs of wealth and social status; they are simply luxuries. They cannot possibly be regarded as necessities—not when comparable apparel can be made of cotton or a synthetic fabric. Yet countless animals are being killed for the very profitable business of marketing these symbols of wealth and status. The victims usually meet their deaths in one of two ways: They are hunted down and bludgeoned to death with clubs or they are snared in one of the cruelest devices ever invented, the steel jaw trap.

DEATH BY THE CLUB

The victims of death by clubbing are young male seals, known in the sealing industry as bachelor pups. Females are spared, for the industry needs them for further breeding. Males are not required in great number for breeding because each usually serves as a husband to "harems" of three to over forty cows. Some males have harems of over one hundred cows.

Several varieties of seal inhabit the world's waters. The type most hunted today for its skin is the northern fur seal. Its soft and short fur is the source of the widely popular sealskin coat. The northern fur seal ranges through the Pacific Ocean from Southern California to

Ranched mink fur pelts await inspection by
buyers during a fur auction in New York City
in 1985. According to a company spokesman, the
furs—minks, fox, beaver, raccoon, and others—were
sold for a total of $25 million to $30 million.

*A newborn harp seal pup on the ice in the
Gulf of St. Lawrence, Canada. The white pelts
of the pups have been commercially marketed
in the past, but through the efforts of
environmentalists, seal hunts
have been reduced considerably.*

the Bering Strait and into the Arctic Ocean. Though a marine animal, it comes ashore to breed. Its major breeding grounds—called rookeries—are the Pribilof Islands off the coast of Alaska, the Commander (Komandorski) Islands near the Soviet Union's Kamchatka peninsula, and the Kuril Islands north of Japan.

For centuries Eskimos have hunted the northern fur seal for food and clothing. Beginning in the 1700s, white men joined the hunt, tracking down this graceful sea creature for its fur, blubber, meat, and bones, all of which were put to commercial use. The white hunters went after both the male and the female, at sea and in the rookeries. So greedy was the search that the animals were threatened with extinction (a danger that some seal groups elsewhere were likewise facing at the hands of the sealing industry). In the mid-nineteenth century, there were about 2.5 million fur seals in the herds at the Pribilof Islands and more than 1 million at the Commander Islands. By 1897 the hunters had reduced these two populations to about 600,000, and by 1911 the Pribilof herds had been cut to a mere 125,000.

Matters, however, took a turn for the better in 1911: Four nations—the United States, Canada, Japan, and Russia—entered an agreement aimed at allowing the herds to repopulate themselves and thus save the sealing industry. The agreement was directed principally against the taking of the animals from the sea, because so many females were gathered up and killed in the process. Commercial sealers were prohibited from sea hunting above 30 degrees North latitude. All hunting was to be limited to the island rookeries—where the males could be singled out for death—and was to be strictly regulated.

The agreement remains in effect to this day. It has enabled the northern fur herds to renew themselves until they again number in the millions. The Pribilof herds have multiplied from the 125,000 of 1911 to a current estimate of over 1.5 million.

Though safeguarded from outright annihilation by the agreement, the northern fur seals are still killed in great numbers. Pribilof hunting, which is conducted under the supervision of the U.S. Fish and Wildlife Service, averages 30,000 pelts a year and has totaled as many as 60,000 a year at times. Once processed for sale, the pelts range in price from $50 to $170 each, with the price depending on an individual fur's quality. The average price per pelt is $100. Five to eight pelts are needed for a sealskin coat.

The northern fur seals abandon the sea and arrive at the rookeries in the spring, with the males coming ashore on the beaches in May, followed by the females in June. The cows that arrive pregnant from the preceding year's breeding (the seal's gestation period lasts eleven months) give birth to their young and then breed again. The cows nurture their pups until September. Then the herds take to the sea once more.

The sealers arrive for their annual hunt in July. The United States limits the catch on the Pribilof Islands to three-year-old bachelors. This limit is imposed because younger and older seals are of little commercial value and their destruction is seen as wasteful of life. The coats of the younger seals are too small for use, while those of the older ones are too coarse.

The hunt begins when U.S. Fish and Wildlife officials come ashore, estimate the size of the herd, and then mark one bachelor for every forty three-year-old females. The marking is done by clipping off some fur. These marked animals are to be spared from death so that they can later breed their harems. The killing of the remaining three-year-old males then takes place at night.

The males lend a helping hand in their destruction. It is their habit to move away from the herd after dark and sleep by themselves. The hunters surround the sleepers and awaken them for the push inland to the killing grounds. The animals are urged along in groups numbering from 1,000 to 3,000; on arrival at the grounds, they are divided into units of twenty to fifty. The hunters now walk in with their clubs and pick out the unmarked three-year-olds. Death comes when the victims are struck with a blow to a soft spot in the skull.

Far to the east, in the Canadian Arctic and stretching across the Atlantic Ocean and Arctic Ocean to the Scandinavian countries and the Soviet Union, other types of seal are hunted. Upward of 30,000 ringed seals are killed yearly by Eskimo and white hunters in northern Canada. The Greenland seal, which breeds on ice floes and is sought after for the white fur covering of its pups, is hunted along the eastern coast of Canada and the northern coast of the Soviet Union and at Jan Mayen Island, north of Iceland. Some of these seals die by the club; others are shot with rifles.

The killing of so many seal varieties has angered advocate groups everywhere, among them Greenpeace (an international organization concerned not only with animal welfare but also about all threats to the environment) and the New York-based Fund for Animals. In 1979 the Fund for Animals infuriated Canadian sealers when it sent a ship into Arctic waters to safeguard a group of white-coated pups from destruction. Eight volunteers went ashore from the ship one night and saved the lives of four hundred animals by painting them with a red dye that did them no physical harm but made their pelts unusable for sale.

THE STEEL JAW TRAP

Canada and the United States are rich in game. Fur-bearing animals are commercially hunted on land and in fresh water throughout both countries, with, as you will recall, at least 13 million losing their lives each year. Most are caught with a device that trappers and animal advocates alike regard as vicious: the steel jaw trap,

*A volunteer from the Fund for Animals
sprays red dye on a seal pup,
rendering its pelt unusable for sale.*

which is also known as the leghold trap. Though box snares and nets are used in some places, the American Fur Institute estimates that 87 percent of all fur animals caught in the United States are the victims of the steel jaw trap.

First developed in the United States in the 1830s, the trap consists of two arcing bands of steel that are joined at their ends by hinges. The bands lie flat and form a rough circle when the trap is open (some traps have the shape of a figure 8 when open); at the center of the circle is a spring with a trigger attachment. The whole idea is to have an animal wander into the trap and step on the trigger. The trigger activates the spring, which snaps the two steel bands together as if they were monster jaws. The victim is caught, usually by a leg or paw and is held fast. To keep its prisoner from dragging it away and disappearing into the bushes, the trap is usually staked to the ground or chained to a tree or tree stump.

The trap is not intended to kill and does so only on occasion. Rather, tearing into the skin and often breaking the leg, it locks the animal in place until the fur trapper comes to see what it has snared. The victim must wait hours and sometimes days or even a week or so (especially in bad weather) before the trapper is able to make that visit. All the while the prisoner endures weather changes, faces the danger of hungry animals, and struggles to break free, suffering excrutiating pain as the steel jaws dig deeper into the flesh with every movement. Death finally comes with a blow by the trapper's club. When a water animal such as a beaver is caught, the agony lasts for about fifteen minutes before the victim drowns.

During its long wait, the animal suffers not only pain but also starvation and thirst. Often it tries to break free by chewing off the trapped leg or paw. On investigating dead victims, researchers have found no food in the stomach, but bits of fur, bones, and broken teeth instead—all evidence of the panic-stricken attempt to escape. Should the animal finally break away, it usually crawls off into the underbrush to die of its wound or lack of food and water. At one time sharp teeth were cut along the edges of the steel bands to make certain that the animal was securely held, but they were discarded and the edges of the bands left smooth when it was found that the teeth sometimes cut so deeply that the animal was better able to chew or pull itself free.

On top of all else, the steel jaw trap is an indiscriminate device. Its fur-bearing targets are not the only thing it catches, for its jaws snap shut just as quickly when some other creature—a sheep, dog, or deer—wanders into it. The trapper calls these animals trash. They make up a terrible percentage—in fact, the greatest percentage—of the trap's victims. For every fur-bearing victim, about three "trash" animals are caught, a fact that drastically alters the total number of animals said to be trapped in the U.S. and Canada each year. The total of at least 13 million does not include the "trash" animals; they raise it to about 39 million.

GETTING RID
OF THE TRAP

Because of its cruel nature, attempts have been made to rid the hunting world of the trap and replace it with snares said to be more humane. Box snares and nets have been suggested and, as you know, are used in various locales.

A device widely recommended as a replacement is the Conibear trap. This snare, which is similar to the steel jaw trap and bears the name of its trapper inventor, is designed to grab the victim at the neck and bring instant death by breaking the neck or the backbone. But animal advocates are quick to point out a problem with the Conibear: The trap does not instantly kill its every victim. It comes in several sizes and, should a large model catch a small animal—or a small Conibear snare

A dog accidentally caught in the grip of a steel jaw trap

a large prey—it will only bring pain by grabbing some part of the body other than the neck. On top of all else, the advocates greet the Conibear with the same scorn shown all "humane" methods of killing. Killing, no matter how quickly done, is still killing and in no way can ever be described as humane.

The Conibear has also failed to gain widespread approval among trappers. It is more expensive than the steel jaw trap and is far more complicated to put in place. There is the ever-present danger that the trapper himself will be snared and injured while setting it up.

Advertised as another more humane method of securing animal pelts is the fur farming, or fur ranching, system. Here, instead of being caught in a trap, the animals are raised much as they are in factory farming, in crowded cages or other small enclosures. Foxes, minks, and chinchillas are among the fur bearers most commonly raised on farms today. They are forced to undergo breeding experiments with which farmers have developed a wide variety of unusual fur colors, including many pastel shades. When the time comes for sale, the animals are slaughtered. The smaller victims are often suffocated to death by having their heads placed in jars containing chloroform, which "humanely" renders the victims unconscious.

Animal advocates say that there is but one way to be rid of the steel jaw trap: Its use must be banned worldwide. They are not alone in their feelings. The trap has already been banned by governments in every part of the globe. In all, more than seventy governments, though not insisting that fur trapping itself be halted, have recognized the trap's cruel nature and have required that more humane devices—for example, box snares and nets—be used in its place. Representing nations of all sizes, these governments make up a very impressive list:

Austria
Bahrain
Bangladesh
Belize
Benin
Botswana
Brazil
British West Indies
Burundi
Cameroon
Chile
Colombia
Costa Rica
Cuba
Cyprus
Denmark
Dominican Republic
Equatorial Guinea
Gabon
Gambia
German Federal Republic
Ghana
Great Britain
Greece
Guyana
Hong Kong
Hungary
India
Ireland
Israel
Italy
Ivory Coast
Jamaica
Jordan
Liberia
Liechtenstein

Malawi
Malaysia
Maldives
Mali
Mauritania
Monaco
Morocco
Mozambique
Netherlands
Nicaragua
Niger
Nigeria
Norway
Panama
Philippines
Portugal
Senegal
Seychelles
Singapore
Sri Lanka
Swaziland
Sweden
Switzerland
Tanzania
Thailand
Tobago
Togo
Trinidad
Tunisia
Uganda
United Arab Emirates
Upper Volta
Zaire
Zambia
Zimbabwe

Missing from the list are the fur-rich United States, Canada, and Soviet Union. Though not outlawed nationwide in Canada and the United States, the steel jaw trap is banned in certain of their areas. It cannot be used, for example, in the Canadian province of British Columbia, nor is it legal in the states of Florida, Hawaii, and Massachusetts nor parts of New Jersey. It is banned in these states owing to an anti-trap campaign that animal advocates launched back in 1923 and that continues to this day.

For years U.S. legislators discussed possible laws to ban the steel jaw trap nationwide. To date, however, no such ban has been enacted. The efforts at such passage have been thwarted, in the main, by pressures exerted on congressional leaders by the fur industry and sportsmen. (As we will soon see, most American trappers are amateurs who hunt down the animals for fun and some extra money.) Many states that have attempted to outlaw the trap within their own borders have met the same opposition.

A new anti-trap bill, however, is now being considered by the U.S. Congress. It strikes at the trap by barring from interstate commerce (commerce carried on among the states) any furs or leathers that come from a country or state permitting its use. The U.S. advocate organization Friends of Animals has developed a law that it hopes to see used as a model for states considering a ban within their borders. The model bill would prohibit anyone from setting a steel jaw trap and from manufacturing, selling, importing, transporting, or obtaining furs from any animal snared by the trap. It would impose a fine of not less than $100 and not more than $500 for a first offense; a second offense would bring a fine of $500 to $1000, with subsequent offenses entailing fines of up to $5000 and the possibility of a six-month prison sentence.

Many advocates think that both the federal bill and the model state bill have a good chance of passage should they ever come to a vote. The chances of passage are considered good because of the growing concern felt by the public for the trapped animals, a concern that is being voiced in angry charges not only against the trap itself but against the entire trapping industry.

ANGRY CHARGES

Animal advocates have long accused the trapping industry of endangering one furred species after another with extinction. They point to the state of Ohio as a case in point. Trappers wiped out the state's beaver population in the 1830s and ended such trapping there for a century. It was not until the 1930s that beaver spread to Ohio from Pennsylvania and New York in sufficient numbers to allow trapping to begin again. Today Ohio supplies the fur trade with well over a million pelts from various animals.

The advocates further accuse the fur industry of being a useless one, one that does nothing but profit from the vanity of some of the world's affluent people. To show how costly this "commerce in vanity" is to the fur-bearing population, Friends of Animals recently issued a fact sheet listing the number of animals that are sacrificed to make a single fur coat 40 inches (102 cm) in length.

Coat Fur	Target Animals Used in Coat	"Trash" Animals Killed for Coat
Coyote	16	48
Lynx	18	54
Mink	60	180
Opossum	45	135
Red fox	42	126

Raccoon	40	120
Sable	50	150
Seal	8	—
Muskrat	50	150
Beaver	15	45

The fur industry answers the advocate charges by saying that it provides jobs for many people—trappers, tailors, shippers, and store salespeople. It also argues that it helps control the animal populaton: It keeps the fur bearers from multiplying too fast and weeds out undesirable animals by snaring old, weak, and sick victims, thus making life better for the rest and enabling the healthier animals to flourish. It further claims that trapping helps control the spread of animal diseases that pose a threat for humans, such as rabies.

These claims are met by angry contradictions from animal advocates. Ann Herrington, the president of Friends of Animals, recently commented on the industry's employment picture. In a letter written to state legislators across the country, she stated that fur manufacturing in the United States has declined in recent years and now employs fewer than 4,000 people, most of them located in New York City. The letter went on to explain that most of the fur-manufacturing industry has moved to Asia and Europe and that the export of American pelts is now massive.

As for the trappers themselves, the advocates cite the U.S. Census Bureau, which sets the number of professional American trappers at a mere 1,000. Both the trappers and the workers in manufacturing comprise a miniscule percentage of the nation's employed people. The advocates contend that the bulk of U.S. trapping is done by amateurs—sportsmen who earn extra dollars with their steel jaw traps.

United Animal Defenders, an energetic American

advocate group, states that children do the most trapping. In the leaflet *Trapping Facts*, the Defenders report that "few states have minimum age limits for trappers and any child may set a trap and neglect it when he loses interest. In Ohio, any child ten years old or more, may trap and hunt. No proof of owning a license is required when purchasing leghold traps." Much fur farming is also said to be in the hands of young people.

And what of the claim that the industry supplies a needed control of the animal population? Friends of Animals, in its booklet *A Time to Choose*, replies:

> Nonsense. Any expert who is familiar with animals in their natural habitat knows that food supply, climate and animals themselves do an excellent job of achieving natural balance. The trouble always comes when man intrudes, by destroying natural conditions or by deciding that nature needs help, which means killing off some animals.

In reply to the industry argument that trapping helps to control animal disease, United Animal Defenders contends that trapping actually has little to do with disease but is dictated by the market price of the animal pelts. *Trapping Facts* contains these comments:

> Skunks are particularly susceptible to and carriers of rabies, but owing to the current sale price of their fur of about $2, they are rarely trapped intentionally. On the other hand, bobcats are heavily trapped even though they are seldom found to carry rabies. . . . Leghold traps are baited, but an animal suffering rabies will not eat.

Much advocate anger is directed against the federal and state wildlife agencies that allow widespread trapping and the use of the steel jaw trap. These agencies join the fur industry in saying that trapping is beneficial because it helps control the animal population and reduce the risk of widespread animal disease. The agencies also give financial support to the trapping and hunting of animals that prey on farm crops and ranch animals. In the western United States these activities have seen wolves and coyotes not only trapped but also poisoned, and wild horses and burros have been rounded up because they forage on land needed for cattle grazing.

The advocates, using the same answers that are directed at the industry, contend that the federal and state agencies are merely protecting the highly profitable fur business, are causing anguish to safeguard farms and ranches when other less painful methods could be employed, and are using vast amounts of the taxpayer's money to do so.

A Time to Choose cites several examples of how federal tax money is spent for trapping. Representative of them all is the following program of animal control:

> The U.S. Department of the Interior hires 437 trappers and supplies them with 20,000 steel jawed traps, all at your expense, to kill wild animals which live on public lands. It publishes a widely distributed pamphlet, "Trapping Tips," aimed at school groups and the general public. "Trapping of furbearing animals for wholesome outdoor recreation and a source of additional income for farm youngsters has been popular since the founding of our country," the pamphlet says. Having equated the inhumane slaughter of animals with the Declaration of Independence, the pamphlet goes on to praise steel

jawed traps as useful weapons. In addition . . . the Department spends over $5,000,000 of your tax money each year for a so-called predator program that relies largely on steel-jawed traps.

THE CALL FOR
PUBLIC ACTION

Such advocate groups as Friends of Animals are calling for widespread public support of the proposed federal anti-trap law and state laws fashioned along the lines of the Friends' model bill. Everyone is asked to write to his or her federal and state representatives and urge the passage of these bills. These bills will, in the minds of many advocates, mark the first steps along the road to greatly reducing or even eliminating fur trapping in the United States.

CHAPTER SEVEN

THE ENTERTAINERS: THE HUNTER'S PREY

Of the many works that animals have performed for humans, one of the greatest has been their service as "entertainers." They have pleased us in zoos, circuses, and motion pictures; they have excited us in sporting events ranging from horse races to rodeos; they have served as targets for the sportsman's gun, trap, and fishhook; and, for countless people everywhere, they have provided pleasure and companionship as pets.

A point stressed in earlier chapters must be repeated here. As is true of laboratory and farm animals, not every animal used for our entertainment has been mistreated or killed, but, as is so true of science and farming, the sad fact is that many of our entertainments do involve terrible abuse. It is an abuse that is especially prevalent in the three areas to be discussed in this and the following chapter. This chapter concerns the animal as the target of the hunter. The next chapter will discuss animals as performers in the sports and entertainment industries and as pets in the home.

THE HUNTER'S PREY

According to recent government statistics, there are an estimated 16.5 million people with hunting licenses in the United States today, plus another 3 million to 5 million who hunt without bothering to obtain a license. Their sport has always outraged animal advocates and great segments of the public, all of whom see it as a brutal activity that should not be called a sport at all.

As animal advocate groups angrily remind everyone, a sport always involves at least two parties in competition with each other. The participants know that they are in a competition and are usually well equipped for it. How then, the advocates ask, can something be called a sport when one of the participants is without the necessary equipment and does not even know what is going on? As it minds its own business, the animal is silently tracked down and then, often without even the chance to see its attacker, is felled from a distance by buckshot or a bullet.

And how, the groups add, can any activity whose purpose is death possibly be called a sport?

The American sports hunter is interested in some thirty animal species. Made up of mammals and fowl, they are known as game animals and include bear, bighorn sheep, bobcats, deer, ducks, geese, mountain lions, and pheasants. Some game animals, such as ducks and deer, are stalked in the wilds; a number of their species have been gunned into extinction over the years, among them the passenger pigeon, the Eastern elk, and the plains wolf.

Others, especially pheasants and wild turkeys, are reared on hunting farms, where they are usually raised in cages or pens until ready to be hunted. Then they are released to be killed by the farm's customers. In some instances the farm operators place the pheasant and turkey eggs throughout the area. The hunters arrive soon after the eggs have hatched. Of the farm-raised animals, the pheasant is not native to North America. It was first imported from Asia for the hunter's pleasure. On being released from its pen, it finds itself in an area where it cannot survive. Its sole purpose is to die by the hunter's gun.

THE HUNTING GROUNDS

Game animals are hunted on both private and public lands. However, much—if not most—hunting in the United States is done on public lands. These lands consist of state and federal parks, forests, and, amazingly, wildlife refuges—areas that have been specially set aside for the protection of the animals against destruction.

Animal advocates, while deploring hunting on private property, are particularly outraged by the use of public lands for hunting. As they see it, the taxes paid by the entire nation are being used—against the wishes of many taxpayers—for the pleasure of relatively few people. The country's 16.5 million licensed hunters, plus those without licenses, make up less than 10 percent of the U.S. population, which is now estimated at just over 230 million.

Much advocate anger is concentrated on the hunter's use of federal lands. The anger here centers on the fact that many of these lands, owing to the work of such early conservationists as President Theodore Roosevelt, were originally set aside as wildlife refuges. The purpose was to save the many animals that were being threatened with extinction as the developing nation pushed westward ever deeper into the wilds. Over the years the federal government has continued to establish wildlife refuges, and today they number more than 400, covering upward of 86 million acres (34 million ha) within the continental United States, Hawaii, and such U.S. holdings as American Samoa.

But, over those same years, the government has treated many of these lands as if it had forgotten that they are refuges. Some have been used for natural gas exploration, farming, and lumbering and, since 1949, a number have been opened to hunters (and trappers). As Karen O'Connor reports in her book *Sharing the Kingdom: Animals and Their Rights*, these openings have been greatly accelerated in recent times. She states that from 1981 to 1983 thirty-five refuges were made available for the hunting of one or more animals. The 1980s have seen fourteen opened to trappers. Of the 220 refuges presently used for sports hunting, 172 are the homes of endangered species. More than half the refuges are now open to hunters (and trappers).

The result has been tragic for the animals. Karen O'Connor reports that in 1982 hunters killed 386,326 animals living on United States refuges. Among their number were 219 swans and over 225,000 ducks. Some 85,473 mammals were shot down. They included bobcats, mountain goats, bighorn sheep, and the tiny Sitka deer. She goes on to say that another twelve thousand animals were crippled and left to die from injuries, exposure, and starvation. Over half a million animals were trapped on federal lands between 1980 and 1985, mostly with the leghold trap.

In recent years the federal government has opened other of its grounds to hunting and trapping. A number of the country's national parks, especially the newly established ones, have been made available to the sports hunter. Traditionally, hunting and trapping have been forbidden in national parks, a prohibition that is being sidestepped by calling some facilities "national recreation areas" rather than "national parks." Hunting and trapping are then allowed, because they are regarded as recreational activities.

The federal government has not been alone in opening its lands to the hunter. Many states have been doing the same thing with their wildlife refuges, parks, and forests. Today state fish and game agencies supervise wildlife programs on more than 600 million acres (240 million ha) of public land, including land designated for U.S. military use. Most of these programs permit and even encourage hunting. In all, at least 700 million acres (280 million ha) of state and federal land are available today for hunting and trapping.

TAX MONIES

Each year the federal and state governments spend vast amounts of money on public-land programs, many of which, as we will soon see, do much to promote hunting. An estimated $23.5 million is spent annually by the states, and at the federal level the U.S. Department of the Interior spends about $500 million a year. (The Department of the Interior is the agency in charge of U.S. public lands.) Other federal agencies, among them the Department of Agriculture and the Soil Conservation Service, also provide funds for public-land programs.

Furthermore, the federal government annually pays about $60 million to $65 million to help the states promote hunting. This money is obtained from the U.S. excise tax that customers pay when purchasing firearms and ammunition. At one time the excise tax funds were placed in the nation's general treasury, but things changed in 1937 with the congressional passage of a law that required the funds to be distributed among the states. That the distribtuion is meant to promote hunting is seen in the fact that the share received by each state is proportional to the number of hunters in that state. To date, more than $1.3 billion in excise taxes have gone to the states.

Just how are these various tax moneys used in great part to promote hunting? Friends of Animals provides what may be the best answer of all in its leaflet *Dressed to Kill*. The leaflet lists a series of statistics issued in 1975 by the U.S. Department of the Interior. In that year, more than a half million acres (200,000 ha) of federal and state lands were drastically altered in programs that were obviously of no possible value to the nation's countless nature lovers—all the campers, hikers, picnickers, sightseers, and outdoor photographers. They benefitted only the hunter and trapper. Here is what happened:

422,868 acres (169,147 ha) were burned. The burning was done to allow the sunlight to reach the ground and encourage the growth of vegetation there as food for a prime hunting target— the deer. Food at ground level is necessary because, as hunters say, "deer can't climb trees." With nourishment now so readily at hand, the deer population would more quickly multiply and provide the hunter with additional prey.

18,094 acres (7,238 ha) were clear-cut, again to provide the deer with more food at ground level.

35,415 acres (14,166 ha) were sprayed with Agent Orange and other defoliants. The purpose here was the same as above.

126,375 acres (50,550 ha) were bulldozed. Once more, the purpose was the same.

599,526 acres (239,810 ha) were flooded to attract migrating geese and ducks for the hunters' guns.

32,640 miles (52,550 km) of road were constructed in the wilderness to give sportsmen better access to the hunting grounds.

Advocates point out that all this work has helped the hunters by increasing the number of game animals. But it has spelled disaster for other species—the nongame animals—that make their homes in the affected areas. Among those injured, left homeless, driven away, or killed have been owls, raccoons, lizards, snakes, and countless birds and insects, all of them important links in the chain of life and vital elements in the richness and balance of the nation's ecological system. Nongame animals make up more than 90 percent of all U.S. wildlife. Some species have been rendered extinct in the name of hunting, the advocates charge, while others are being pushed along the road to extinction.

If the above example is not enough, others can be added to the list. One is the U.S. Department of Agriculture's "Public Access Program." With a budget of at least $1.5 million a year, it pays farmers who allow hunters, trappers, fishermen, and hikers to use their lands. The Department of Agriculture defends this program by saying that the hunters and trappers help control the wildlife that preys on farm animals. The states and the federal government support programs that plant food for game animals, maintain ponds to attract waterfowl targets, stock lakes with fish, and provide loans to sports groups for the construction and repair of housing for sportsmen.

WHY SO MUCH TAX MONEY FOR HUNTING?

The states and the federal government defend their programs that promote hunting on several counts. Basically, they depend on the same argument that is used to justify trapping. They claim that the programs help control the animal population by weeding out the sick and infirm and thus giving healthier animals a better chance to flourish. They go on to claim that the programs also do much to rid the land of animals that prey on other wildlife and on farm and ranch animals. There is also the argument that the taxes paid by the hunters themselves do much to support the programs. As taxpayers, the hunters then have a right to pursue their sport on the public lands.

Animal advocates scoff at these claims. Their basic argument is that the states and the federal government are pressured into hunter programs by influential sports organizations (chief among them is the National Wildlife Federation, an organization representing a number of hunting and trapping clubs) and the manufacturers of firearms, ammunition, hunting gear, and all the camping equipment that makes the hunter's life comfortable. Furthermore, so the advocates argue, many of the people in charge of our public lands are themselves hunters and thus sympathetic to the programs.

The advocates have an answer for each of the claims, beginning with the one that the programs help control the animal population. Like the claim itself, the reply is the same as that given for trapping: Humans are not needed for this work. Nature itself—through the weather and the available food supply—does a more than adequate job of animal population control on its own.

There are several advocate replies to the claim that the programs enable healthier animals to flourish by weeding out the weak and infirm. A major one concerns that prime target, the deer. The advocates charge that hunters invariably look for the strongest bucks to fetch home as trophies. Instead of leaving the strong to flourish, they leave the weak, a fact that results in weaker future generations. According to Friends of Animals,

*A hunter poised as he draws
his bow on an eight-point buck*

Pennsylvania serves as a fine illustration here. Deer have always been widely hunted in the state, and today they are smaller and weaker than they were at the beginning of this century.

The advocates accuse the hunters of not caring about the best animals of all species, but only about those species that offer the most attractive targets. A case in point is the white-tail deer. As estimated by Friends of Animals, there are some 12 million white-tail deer in the United States today. White-tail deer numbered about half a million at the opening of the century. This prime target has been encouraged to multiply while other species, especially nongame animals, have been driven to the point of extinction.

And what of the claim that the programs weed out animals that prey on other wildlife and on farm and ranch animals? The animal advocates charge that the predators most sought after are those that stalk game animals. For example, Friends of Animals reports that one predator-control program spread strychnine over the ground in a Georgia public area, the purpose being to kill the raccoons that would feed on wild turkey eggs. The eggs had been placed there by the authorities so that the turkeys, on hatching, could serve as hunting targets.

The claim that the taxes paid by the hunters do much to support the programs brings a derisive snort from advocates. They argue that the nation's 16.5 million hunters cannot possibly pay more than a miniscule share of the $23.5 million spent annually by the states and the $500 million spent per year by the U.S. Department of Interior, plus the millions more handed out by other federal agencies. Nor can the hunters' tax payments make up more than a tiny percentage of the $2.3 billion dollars that the federal government recently spent to acquire new national parks, forests, and wildlife refuges. In all, the hunter programs are being mainly paid for by the public at large, 93 percent of whom do not hunt. Included among their number are the 120 million people who visit our national parks yearly armed with only a camera and a love of nature.

On a more specific matter, the advocates point to the federal excise taxes (for the purchase of firearms and ammunition) that are annually distributed to the states. Friends of Animals, using 1978 as a sample year, shows that very little of this money actually comes from hunters. In that year $60 million was paid in excise taxes. There were an estimated 50 million gun owners in the country at that time, of whom only 14 million were licensed hunters. This meant that the hunters themselves paid only about $16 million of the $60 million total. Most of the money came from target shooters and from people who purchased guns for protection or other purposes. In all, then, the hunters are paying only an extremely small share of all the various tax monies that go into the nation's public lands and public-land programs; yet, so the advocates charge, their sport is reaping great benefits from those lands and killing countless animals in the process.

A final derisive snort from the advocates is reserved for the claim that the hunters' taxes help pay for important programs to protect endangered species. In all, less than 2 percent of all the tax money used for public-lands programs is allocated to work on behalf of the nation's many endangered species.

WHAT CAN YOU
DO TO HELP?

In answer to this question, Friends of Animals offers a number of suggestions, some of which you can follow as a young person and all of which you can later follow as an adult. Appearing in several fact sheets issued by Friends, the suggestions include the following:

Ostracize hunters and trappers from your social life. Don't patronize stores and services owned by hunters and trappers.

Buy a few shares in timber and paper corporations. In accordance with the company by-laws, submit a proposal that hunting and trapping be banned in forests owned by the company. Attend the public stockholders' meeting, state your case, and win a favorable vote. Stress that the fees paid to a company by hunting and trapping clubs for use of its property make up only a small amount of its annual earnings.

Convince farmers and other landowners to post their lands with signs forbidding hunting and trapping.

Work for the repeal of the law (it's called the Pittman–Robertson Act) that requires the federal government to distribute to the states the excise taxes collected for gun and ammunition purchases. Urge your federal legislators to have these millions of dollars placed back in the General Treasury so that they can be of service to the entire public.

Urge your federal and state legislators to work for programs that will protect all the nation's wildlife, both game and nongame.

Talk to your friends about what hunting and trapping are doing to our wildlife. Enlist their help in putting an end to the killing.

If you can take some of these steps now—and all of them later on as an adult—you will make a major contribution to reducing or even ending what animal advocates have always seen as widespread and legal murder. It is, in their eyes, a crime that must be stopped if the nation truly believes in the rights of animals and truly wishes to preserve our wildlife from extinction.

CHAPTER EIGHT

THE ENTERTAINERS: PERFORMERS AND PETS

It is the dream of many young people to find a place for themselves in professional sports or entertainment, perhaps as football or baseball players, television performers, or motion picture stars. They know that success in these areas can bring great rewards in money, fame, and personal satisfaction, and they train hard to prepare for the field of their choice.

THE ANIMAL PERFORMERS

Such, however, is not the fate of the animals that find themselves in the sports and entertainment worlds. Without having any say in the matter, they are turned into competitors or performers by their masters. A few—such as the collie Lassie (actually the Lassie role was filled by several dogs)—win fame and are given loving care, in great part because they are such fine money earners. For the majority, however, the performing life means pain and suffering. Let us look at what happens to them.

In Sports

Race horses receive injections of the anti-inflammatory and pain-killing drug Butazoladin so that they can run when lame or injured. Greyhound dogs are trained for racing, but only a few of them ever live to compete on a track: United Animal Defenders reports that approximately 80 percent of these dogs fail to meet their trainers' requirements and are either killed, sold off for laboratory experimentation, or turned into constant breeding machines. The average racing career of a greyhound lasts four years, after which it too usually suffers any of the above fates.

Dog racing is a lethal sport for other animals as well. When in competition, the greyhounds chase a mechanical rabbit around the track. Live rabbits have been outlawed in competition, but they—and kittens—are widely used in training, with the rabbits frequently being tied by their hind legs to a mechanical device that whips them along as the dogs run in pursuit. To encourage greater speeds in the future, the dogs are allowed to catch the rabbit at the end of a training session and usually chew it to death. According to United Animal Defenders, there are some 20,000 registered greyhounds in the United States. The group says that if a minimum of five rabbits are used per year in the training of each dog, then at least 100,000 rabbits are brutally killed annually. This figure does not include the rabbits used to train the 80 percent of the dogs that fail to become registered for competition.

Though outlawed in various areas of the United States, countless pit bulldog fights and cockfights still take place, with the spectators gathering in rural barns and city basements to see the battles, which are usually fought to the death. The fighting cocks are routinely equipped with steel claws with which to rip each other open. In such countries as Spain and Mexico, millions of fans quite legally watch splendid animals destroyed by the matador's sword in bullfights.

Under the Big Top

Circus elephants are trained, often with whippings, to balance themselves on one foot, a feat altogether contrary to their nature and one of tremendous strain, considering their great weight. Lions and tigers, whose natures call for them to be hunting in the wilds, are kept in cages that give them hardly any room to move about and exercise. Bengal tigers are afraid of fire but are forced to jump through flaming hoops. Bears and dogs, though clumsy and uncomfortable when standing upright, are made to pedal bicycles or walk for extended periods on their hind legs.

For the Camera

Cattle have been made to stampede for motion picture action sequences. Horses and sheep have been driven over cliffs and have plunged to the water far below as cameras have whirred. Animals have actually been shot and killed—rather than sedated—in scenes depicting their deaths. Film crews have admitted that it was simpler and less expensive to destroy the animals than to try sedation or some other means to simulate their deaths.

Horses are among the most widely used of film stunt animals and, as such, they have long been among the most abused. Forced on them time and again has been one particularly nasty stunt: the sudden fall, when their riders are "shot" by enemy gunslingers. The stunt is performed by means of "running W's," two ropes that stretch down from the saddle and are attached by clamps to the front hooves of the horse. As the horse is moving at a full gallop, the rider activates the ropes with a trigger device. The ropes pull back and the horse crashes to the ground.

Ever since a horse was killed during the filming of the 1939 western *Jesse James*, the American Humane Association has worked to protect motion picture animals. The horse died when it was made to gallop along a greased plank that was suddenly pulled out from under it, causing it to plunge from a 40-foot (12-m) cliff. Today the association's Hollywood office and its director—former actress Carmelita Pope—check closely to see that no cruelties are inflicted on animal actors in any film. The association reports a constantly increasing cooperation on the parts of producers and film crews.

In the Zoo
Zoo animals, fed regularly by their keepers and lazing in the sun as visitors watch them with delight, are thought to have the easiest lives of all the performers, but their lot is actually one of the worst. While there are some excellent and modern zoos in the United States and elsewhere, animal advocates are constantly reminding us of the sad conditions still found in far too many facilities. These zoos are outdated and were built with the idea of entertaining the visiting public rather than providing comfort for the animals. In the name of displaying as many animals as possible, they feature cramped accommodations that offer the animals no privacy from the spectators, no feeling of being in their native habitats, and little or no opportunity for exercise. Some zoos keep their animals caged alone or in small groups, even though it is known that some species would be happier in large groups so that they could share the company of their fellow creatures. In all these instances the animals run a high risk of becoming listless, bored, and physically unwell.

Furthermore, the cramped living conditions put the survival of some animal species in danger by ignoring their breeding habits. For example, the lack of privacy discourages breeding in mammal species (such as the polar bear), whose females require complete privacy, not only from spectators but also from other animals, when giving birth. On the other hand, many zoos feature single cages for species (the marmoset and certain foxes among them) whose females need and want the assistance of other females during the birth process.

Many zoos, again in the name of displaying the greatest number of animals possible, accept some species that should never be imprisoned at all because, as is true of the cheetah, they need more space in which to live and roam than can be provided by even the best of modern facilities. Additionally, a number of zoos are known for their inadequate care, often feeding the animals too little, paying scant attention to their ills, and failing to keep stalls and cages properly cleaned of droppings and unused food. These problems have been most often caused by the lack of sufficient public or private financing.

But then there is the matter of outright abuse. Some zoo keepers have been accused of mistreating their animal charges, taunting them and poking them with sticks. Abuse is also seen in the very nature of certain zoos, chiefly the "petting zoos," where children are allowed to fondle the animals; to protect the youngsters, a number of such zoos have the animals' teeth pulled. On top of all else, the way in which so many zoos position their stalls and cages—close to the visitors for better viewing—has resulted in much harm to the animals. For example, an ostrich in a well-known zoo once choked to death on a camera flashbulb tossed into the stall by a visitor. In another instance a deer died after swallowing a balloon and a paper bag.

The plight of the animals is so bad and so widespread that many advocates are urging an end to all zoos. They would like to see the zoos replaced by a growing number of animal parks, refuges, and preserves.

Aware of these feelings and long concerned for the animals, the world's best zoos—such as the excellent San Diego Zoo in Southern California—are working to overcome the many sad and traditional shortcomings.

They are providing spacious display areas that simulate the animals' natural habitats. Some are setting aside grounds away from public view where the animals can breed and give birth. The San Diego Zoo has reserved some 1,800 acres (720 ha) for breeding purposes. Also a growing number of zoos are accepting only those animals able to survive in the local climate; no longer need their charges try to adjust themselves to alien and often fatal climatic conditions. Many are concentrating on displaying fewer species (avoiding those that should not be held captive at all) but in larger groups so that the animals will have ample company of their own kind. In all, these zoos are looking on themselves as animal parks and preserves as well as places for the entertainment and education of the public. Their work marks a major trend toward changing what has too long been the unhappy nature of zoos everywhere. It is to be hoped that this trend will continue until its goal is fully achieved.

A SPECIAL SUFFERING

All the above examples give only a general idea of the suffering endured by the sports and entertainment animals. We can gain greater insight into their suffering by turning our attention to one area that animal advocates find especially vicious: the rodeo.

The rodeo is a business that brings its operators and cowboy contestants millions of dollars a year, a fact made clear by the gate receipts for a week-long rodeo held recently at Salinas, California, $9 million. An especially popular attraction in the western United States, it attracts hordes of spectators who feel they are participating in an exciting and traditional contest that dates back to one of the most romantic eras in the nation's history, the opening of the frontier. According to animal advocates, the truth is that the spectators are watching one of the cruelest sports ever devised by humans. To prove the point, they speak of what happens in the rodeo's three basic events—the rough stock, wrestling and roping, and sideshow events.

Rough Stock Events
These events see broncs—either saddled or bareback—and Brahma bulls ridden out of chutes and into the arena. The animals, twisting, turning, and leaping, try to unseat their riders, who must remain aboard for 8 seconds.

Rodeo operators advertise the broncs as "ornery critters," killers that like nothing better than flinging a rider to the ground. But are these horses really all that mean? In many cases the answer is no, because the animals must often be whipped and prodded into a frenzy so that they will perform as desired. Once a bronc is locked in the chute, it is not unusual to see rodeo hands beat it with their hands, yank its mane, twist its tail, and poke it with metal and wooden sticks. Nor is it unusual to see a bronc stand motionless—stubborn and terrified—when the chute door swings open. At that time some rodeo hand will strike it with an electric prod—often in the rectal area—to force it into action

Also, it is rodeo practice to tie a leather strap—a flank strap, as it is called—around the bronc's middle. The leather is cinched tight in the sensitive area of the abdomen and genitals. Much bronc "orneriness" is simply the animal's frenzied attempt to be rid of excruciating pain. Very often, once the strap is removed, the bronc becomes quiet, calm, and gentle.

The Brahma bulls endure the same beatings and proddings received by the broncs.

Steer Wrestling and Calf Roping
In the first of these events, a steer is discharged from a chute and streaks across the arena with a mounted cow-

boy in pursuit. The rider throws himself from his horse, lands on the steer's neck, and wrestles the animal to the ground by twisting its horns until it is thrown off balance. The event often ends in muscle and bone damage about the steer's neck and down its back.

The second event lets a calf loose for a dash across the arena, again with a mounted cowboy in pursuit. This time, however, the rider lassoes the calf, pulling the animal back into a hard fall, and then dismounts to tie the calf's legs together within a certain number of seconds.

Many rodeo critics see calf roping as the cruelest of all the events. The animal is usually traveling at a speed of 25 to 30 miles (40–50 km) an hour at the time that the lasso circles its neck and abruptly yanks it backward. The pull commonly breaks bones in the calf's neck or back, rips muscle tissue, and causes internal bleeding.

Sideshow Events

Perhaps it can be said that bronc riding and calf roping are Western traditions in that they date back to the days when range hands broke wild horses for saddling and roped calves as part of their daily chores, but there is nothing traditional about the sideshow events. They are, in the minds of animal advocates everywhere, no more than silly exercises in "entertainment."

One sideshow event is steer dressing. Here some cowboys trap a steer in the middle of the arena, wrestle it to the ground, and then force a pair of denim jeans up its legs. A companion event, cow milking, features one rodeo hand twisting a cow's horns to hold the animal in place while his partner roughly draws a few ounces of milk from the animal.

Not only injury but also death is the fate of many rodeo animals. In a recent California rodeo two calves suffered broken legs in the roping event and were sold off for slaughter. Rodeo hands have also had to destroy broncs after the animals suffered broken legs. Nor are

One popular rodeo event is calf roping,
not only painful but also
life-threatening to the calf.

the pain and abuse limited to the arena. Animal advocates charge the rodeo people with shipping the animals from one locale to another in crowded boxcars and then keeping them jammed together in pens and stalls at the rodeo grounds while awaiting their turns to perform.

Putting a Stop to the Pain
There are a number of ways in which you can help put a stop to the pain suffered by the rodeo animals, and by all the animals in sports and entertainment. To begin, the many animal organizations recommend that you refuse to attend any sport or entertainment that features animal cruelty, whether it be a rodeo, a motion picture you are longing to see, or a zoo that your school, church, or club group is planning to visit. These are all enterprises that need your money to prosper; take it away from them and they are in trouble. They will either have to change their ways or go out of business. In either case the animals win.

Many people are not fully aware of the cruelties so often found in sports and entertainments. Those horses that sprawl forward when their riders yank the running W's all seem to be part of the make-believe in an action film and so, in common with the villain who is shot in the big final scene, are easily thought to suffer no real harm. But this is not the case at all. Tell your friends of the pain that is really felt and of the death that is always possible. Have them pass the word on to others. Spreading the word will encourage more and more people to speak out against what is being done. And, as has been said before, help the advocate organizations in their work to end all cruelty wherever it is found. Theirs is a strong voice. Yours will make it stronger still.

ANIMALS AS PETS

No one can say how many animals—from dogs and cats to birds, fish, horses, ponies, lizards, and spiders—are kept as pets throughout the world. All that can be said is that the number is certainly in the hundreds of millions, as is made clear by just one statistic. In U.S. homes today there are close to 90 million of the two most popular pets of all: over 52 million dogs and 36 million cats.

Countless household pets are well tended and treated with kindness, as can be proved by yet another single statistic: Americans spend more than $3 billion every year on pet foods. Added to this amount are what may be countless dollars for collars, flea repellants, medicines, bedding, clothing, and veterinary fees. But just as many pets are abused. Animal advocates speak angrily of animal supply companies that force their cats and dogs to breed constantly and then, in imitation of factory farms, rear the offspring in crowded wire cages until ready for marketing to pet stores and laboratories. And we have all read newspaper accounts of pets being harmed by their owners. Some have been beaten, some burned, some left locked in garages, with inadequate food and water, while their owners have gone on week- or month-long vacations. And some have been left in closed cars to suffocate on hot days.

The Strays: A Tragedy

Though all the above cases are tragic, one of the greatest tragedies of all is the fate suffered by the nation's stray cats and dogs. Left homeless for reasons that we will soon see, there are over 120 million strays in the United States. Of that number, only a lucky one out of about every nine finds its way to one of the country's many public and privately owned animal shelters, hopefully to be adopted there by a loving family. But then only a very lucky two out of ten are usually adopted. What happens to the rest? Some may be in shelters that will sell them for laboratory research. The great bulk are put to death—not because the shelter operators are cruel, but because there is simply not enough room to house all the animals or enough money to feed their ever-increasing numbers. In all, some 14 million strays must be destroyed annually in the United States.

Of those that must be destroyed, many are placed in decompression chambers, from which the air is sucked, causing the animals to die, hopefully in a few seconds, from the lack of oxygen. This procedure is regarded as cruel and is outlawed in many states. Seen as a far more humane means of death is the injection of the chemical sodium pentabarbitol, which induces a deep and fatal sleep. The use of sodium pentabarbitol is endorsed by many animal advocates.

Why are there so many strays? A few are runaways or pets that have been permanently lost during family outings and vacations. Many, however, are the victims of owners who no longer want to take the responsibility for them. Perhaps the animals cost too much to feed. Perhaps they are no longer the cute things they once were when they were kittens and puppies. Whatever the reason, the owners—unlike caring people—do not seek a new family for them or place them in a shelter for adoption; rather, they simply drop the unsuspecting animals off in distant neighborhoods, along roadsides, or in rural areas, all in the hope that they will somehow survive and find a home. Too often the pets are hit and killed by cars or starve to death or they are picked up by the authorities and placed in shelters.

Perhaps most of the strays are the offspring of pets that have been allowed to roam free and breed as they wish. If the pet is a male, the owner will likely not even know the mother of its litter. If the pet is a female, the owner will be unwilling to care for the newborn and will try to give them away (often to strangers who may or may not prove to be kind and responsible owners), hand them over to shelters, or simply abandon them. Many owners, when explaining why they abandoned the pets when there was a shelter nearby, will say that they knew of how so many strays had to be destroyed and therefore felt that abandonment was giving the animals a better chance to live. They were completely wrong.

Easing the Tragedy
Animal advocates say that the tragedy of the strays can be greatly eased and perhaps even ended if everyone took but two steps when purchasing an animal from a pet store or adopting one from a shelter. If you are planning to do so, you should first ask yourself some questions and answer them honestly; they are questions that will show whether you will make a loving or irresponsible owner. Second, once you have chosen your pet, you can work to solve the problem of indiscriminate breeding by having the animal neutered if it is a male and spayed if it is a female.

Alice Herrington, the president of Friends of Animals, has written an informational pamphlet titled *So You Think You Want a Pet?* She recommends the following questions and gives her reasons why they must be asked and honestly answered:

Can you accept the fact that it won't be a baby forever?

An adorable little kitten will fit into your pocket. A cuddly puppy will snuggle into your lap. But they will both became gawky adolescents capable of knocking over breakable objects, getting entangled in people's feet and creating havoc with household routine. Fully grown, they may be much larger than you expected and not nearly as cute as they once were. Animal shelters are full of pets that were rejected once they grew past babyhood.

Are you prepared to give it lifetime care?

When a cat or dog is fully grown, it is still totally dependent upon you for all its needs. You must provide it with food and water, change its litter box or walk it regularly and make sure that it gets sufficient exercise. You are responsible for watching over its health, keeping it clean and taking it to the vet if it shows symptoms of illness. You must maintain discipline so that it does not become a nuisance and you must give it attention and affection so that it remains the loving pet you wanted when you got the animal.

Have you time to feed, exercise and groom it?

Cats usually give themselves enough exercise, but dogs must be taken for walks and runs regularly. Feeding has to be regular and dependable. Grooming is of utmost importance to long-haired breeds, and not for looks alone. If the thick, silky coat isn't combed thoroughly and frequently, it becomes matted and tangled, creating excellent hiding places for fleas and skin disorders. If you don't feel well, or the weather is bad, or you're going on vacation, your pet must still be taken care of.

Can you give it daily care and companionship?

A pet is not a toy to be taken out and played with occasionally, then tucked away until it is wanted again. It is a living creature with a constant need for affection and reassurance. An animal needs daily human contact and attention. If you cannot fill these needs, then you should not have a pet.

Can you afford the financial responsibility of ownership?

Whatever you pay to acquire an animal in the first place is only a drop in the bucket compared to the expenses that are likely to accrue over the lifetime of the pet. In addition to food, there are puppy shots, checkups and vaccinations, veterinarians' fees, licenses and medicines. Unexpected costs may include damage to neighbors' property, legal fees, torn clothing and wear and tear on furniture and carpets.

Herrington also mentions the need for neutering and spaying. Both are simple, inexpensive operations, so simple, in fact, that the animal usually recovers in a day or so. Both are performed with the aid of anesthetics and thus are not painful. Neutering removes the male's testes and spaying removes the female's uterus and ovaries. Animal advocates point out that, contrary to popular belief, the pets do not suffer as humans would from a loss of sexual ability or power. The animals do not become fat or lazy or mean tempered, because, unlike humans, they do not realize that there has been a sexual loss.

Many shelters and animal groups sponsor low-cost or free neutering and spaying programs.

A FINAL NOTE

From the cruelties endured by laboratory animals to those suffered by pets in the home, we have seen them all in these chapters. They are cruelties that anger, shock and embarrass us—embarrass us because they are done by the animal species of which we are members and so seem to reflect on each one of us personally. But we

have every reason to curb our embarrassment. Why? Because there are countless of our kind who would never think of hurting our fellow land, sea, and sky creatures, and in all corners of the world there are countless of our kind working daily to end all the suffering, pain, and death. We cannot be embarrassed by any of them; rather, we can only feel pride for their compassion and their work.

And we can feel pride in our own deep concern for animals, a concern that has prompted both the writing and the reading of this book. We can feel ever-greater pride—plus a great sense of justice done—if we join their ranks and lend our own hands to their efforts. And, indeed, it will be justice done. For the animals do not simply deserve our kind and decent treatment because we are their superiors in some ways and so are greatly responsible for their welfare. Rather, they have a right to our kindness and decency because they are fellow living creatures and fellow sharers of our planet.

*A public demonstration
for animal rights.*

YOUR
HELPING
HAND

Throughout this book, we have talked of ways in which you can personally help end animal abuse and encourage a greater appreciation for the rights of animals. As you know, perhaps the most effective step is to learn about and join one or more of the many organizations working today to protect animals and their rights. To help you take this all-important step, the following is a list of twenty-five organizations dedicated to animal assistance, plus brief descriptions of their basic aims. All these organizations are national in their scope. There are also numerous regional and local groups that deserve your attention and support.

American Fund for Alternatives to Animal Research
175 West 12th Street
Suite 16G
New York, New York 10011

Makes grants available to help laboratory research that does not use animals; issues a newsletter.

American Humane Association
5351 So. Roslyn Street
Englewood, Colorado 80111

Works to prevent cruelty to both animals and children, though deals mostly in pet matters; issues a number of informational publications.

American Society for the Prevention of
  Cruelty to Animals
441 E. 92nd Street
New York, New York 10028

Strives for the humane treatment of domestic and some other animals; investigates cases of cruelty; maintains shelters and hospitals; enforces some animal protection laws; issues a number of informational materials.

Animal Protection Institute of America
P.O. Box 22505
Sacramento, California 94822

Carries out various programs—informational, educational, and research—to encourage the humane treatment of all animals; issues various informational publications.

Animal Welfare Institute
P.O. Box 3650
Washington, D.C. 20007

Seeks humane treatment for animals in laboratory research; issues books and a quarterly report.

Associated Humane Societies
124 Evergreen Avenue
Newark, New Jersey 07114

Dedicated to achieving the humane treatment of some domestic animals; maintains shelters and hospitals; issues a monthly newspaper and other materials.

Beauty Without Cruelty
175 W. 12 Street
New York, New York 10011

Works to end the use of animals in the cosmetics industry (by producing cosmetics tested with nonanimal methods) and to end commercial and sports trapping.

Canadian Federation of Humane Societies
101 Champagne Avenue
Ottawa, Ontario
Canada K1S 4P3

Seeks to reduce the suffering of domestic animals.

Defenders of Wildife
1244 19th Street, N.W.
Washington, D.C. 20036

Dedicated to the protection of all wildlife; issues a bimonthly magazine.

Farm Animal Reform Movement
P.O. Box 70123
Washington, D.C. 20088

Activist organization dedicated to ending the suffering of farm animals.

Friends of Animals
1 Pine Street
Neptune, New Jersey 07753

Works against the abuse of all animals, whether they be wild or domesticated; interested in the control of pet overpopulation; offers low-cost neutering/spaying programs; issues materials on a wide variety of abuses, including those seen in hunting, trapping, scientific and medical research, and factory farming.

Fund for Animals
140 W. 57th Street
New York, New York 10019

Works against the inhumane treatment of most animals; seeks to protect wildlife; issues a newsletter.

Humane Society of the United States
2100 L Street, N.W.
Washington, D.C. 20037

Urges the humane and compassionate treatment of all animals; issues a news magazine for children and a quarterly magazine for adults.

The Institute for the Study of Animal Problems
(Research Division of the Humane Society
   of the United States)
2100 L Street, N.W.
Washington, D.C. 20037

Engages in scientific studies of animal problems; issues a bimonthly journal.

International Network for Religion and Animals
P.O. Box 33061
Washington, D.C. 20033

Educational group relating animal issues to various world religions.

Medical Research Modernization Committee
11 West 60th Street
New York, New York 10023

Seeks the development of research methods not employing animals; publishes various materials.

National Anti-Vivisection Society
100 E. Ohio Street
Chicago, Illinois 60611

Educates the public, through various programs and publications, on the wrongs of animal vivisection; issues various informational materals (booklets, pamphlets, fact sheets) and a bimonthly bulletin.

National Association for the Advancement
  of Humane Education
(Education Division of the Humane Society
  of the United States)
P.O. Box 362
East Haddam, Connecticut 06423

Works to improve human education programs in the nation's schools; issues various materials, including newsletters and curriculum guides.

People for the Ethical Treatment of Animals
P.O. Box 42516
Washington, D.C. 20015

Regarded by many as the most active animal rights organization in the United States; has participated in successful campaigns to close down various federally funded laboratories; lobbies on Capitol Hill to further legislation on the behalf of all animals, including farm animals; maintains chapters throughout the United States.

Physicians Committee for Responsible Medicine
P.O. Box 6322
Washington, D.C. 20015

A network of doctors concerned with addressing the ethical questions raised by animal experimentation; assists members of Congress in developing legislation on the behalf of laboratory animals; uses the expertise of its members to educate legislators and the public on the issue of animals experimentation.

The Society for Animal Protective Legislation
P.O. Box 3719
Georgetown Station
Washington, D.C. 20007

Urges legislation to end the abuse of wildlife; issues various informational materials.

Society for Animal Rights
421 S. State Street
Clarks Summit, Pennsylvania 18411

Strives to end the laboratory use of animals; issues various materials on the suffering endured by laboratory animals.

Student Action Corps for Animals
P.O. Box 15588
Washington, D.C. 20003

A network of students involved in animal issues; assists students who refuse to dissect animals in school laboratories.

United Action for Animals
205 E. 42nd Street
New York, New York 10017

Seeks research methods to replace the use of laboratory animals; works on legislation to protect animals; issues a quarterly report.

United Animal Defenders
P.O. Box 33086
North Royalton, Ohio 44133

Dedicated to the protection of animals; publishes various informational materials.

RECOMMENDED READING LIST

If you would like to read more about animal rights and welfare, the following materials will prove interesting and helpful. They were used in the preparation of this book.

BOOKS

Curtis, Patricia. *Animal Rights: Stories of People Who Defend the Rights of Animals.* New York: Four Winds Press, 1980.

Fox, Michael, and Morris, Richard Knowles. *On the Fifth Day.* Washington, D.C.: Acropolis Books, 1978.

McCoy, Joseph. *In Defense of Animals.* New York: Seabury Press, 1978.

Mason, Jim, and Singer, Peter. *Animal Factories.* New York: Crown, 1980.

Morse, Mel. *Ordeal of the Animals.* Englewood Cliffs, N.J.: Prentice-Hall, 1968.

O'Connor, Karen, *Sharing the Kingdom: Animals and Their Rights.* New York: Dodd-Mead, 1984.

Regan, Tom, and Singer, Peter. *Animal Rights and Human Obligations.* Englewood Cliffs, N.J.: Prentice-Hall, 1976.

Reusch, Hans. *Slaughter of the Innocent.* New York: Bantam Books, 1978.

Rollin, Bernard. E. *Animal Rights and Human Morality.* Buffalo, N.Y.: Prometheus Books, 1981.

Singer, Peter. *Animal Liberation: A New Ethic for Our Treatment of Animals.* New York: Avon Books, 1975.

_____. *In Defense of Animals* (edited by Peter Singer, with chapters by many activists and philosophers). New York: Basil Blackwell, 1985.

NEWSPAPER ARTICLES

Boffey, Philip M. "The Rights of Animals and Requirements of Research." *New York Times,* August 11, 1985.

Petit, Charles. "New Animal Research Center at Stanford." *San Francisco Chronicle,* August 8, 1985.

Robbins, William. "Animal Rights: A Growing Movement in U.S." *New York Times,* June 15, 1984.

MAGAZINE ARTICLES

James, Carollyn. "A Rabbit's-Eye View." *Science 84,* March 1984.

Dunheim, Dee. "What Should Come First . . . The Rabbit or the Egg?" *American Anti-Vivisection Society Bulletin,* Winter 1982–83.

Dusheck, J. "Protesters Prompt Halt in Animal Research." *Scientific News,* July 27, 1985.

Kowinski, William Severine. "One Man's Beef." *New York Daily News Magazine,* April 14, 1985.

BOOKLETS, PAMPHLETS, FACT SHEETS

The following are some of the materials published by various animal protection organizations. These materials are available at a nominal price from the organizations. The names and addresses of the organizations are to be found in the section of this book entitled "Your Helping Hand." Booklets and leaflets are printed below in italics; regular type is used for fact sheets.

Friends of Animals
    The Agony of Fur
    Alternatives to Research on Animals
    The Case Against the LD50 Test
    The Case Against Leghold Traps
    Dressed to Kill
    Factory Farming
    Rodeo Critics Call It "Legalized Cruelty"
    So You Think You Want a Pet?
    A Time to Choose
    Where Do You Stand?
        Facts About the "SPORT" of Hunting
    Who Pays the Tab for Wildlife Conservation?

Medical Research Modernization Committee
    The Case Against the Draize Test

People for the Ethical Treatment of Animals
    Alternatives to the Use of Animals in Experimentation
    Animals Used in War Research
    The Issue: Animal Experimentation
    Testing Cosmetics and Household Products
    Typical Animal Experiments
    What is the L.D. 50 Test?
    What's in Your Meat?
    Animal Rights and the Feminist Connection

The Society for Animal Protective Legislation
Steel Jaw Traps Maim and Cripple Pets

United Animal Defenders
Factory Farming
Greyhound Racing
Trapping Facts

In addition to the above materials, you may wish to read copies of the magazine *Animal's Agenda*. It is the publication most widely read by animal advocates in the United States. Issued ten times a year, the magazine deals with all current animal issues and cases. Its subscription price is $15 per year and it can be obtained by writing to Box 5234, Westport, Connecticut 06881.

INDEX

Rats, 25–26, 32, 33, 63
Religions, 15
Reproduction of animals,
   14–15, 20–21, 26, 74,
   116–18, 124, 127
Revlon, 47, 60
Robbin, William, 53, 55
Rodeo animals, 118–20,
   121, 122
Rollin, Bernard E., 25–26

Scientific advances made
   without animal re-
   search, 35–36
Seal hunting, 82, *84*, 85–
   87, *88*
Singer, Peter, 18–20
Slaughter, 17, 72, 77
Spaying, 15, 127
Specieism, 19
Spira, Henry, 60
Sports, animals in, 114
Steel jaw trap, 89–90, *91*,
   92–95

Strays, 63, 123–27
Subjugation of animals,
   14–16

Tax support for hunting,
   104–7, 109–10, 111
Trapping, commercial,
   81–82
   alternatives to, 90,
   92–95
   opposition to, 92, 94–
   99
   steel jaw trap, 89–90,
   91, 92–95
Trapping, sport, 103–4

United Animal Defenders,
   96–97, 114

Vegetarianism, 15, 21

Wildlife refuges, 102–3

Zoo animals, 116–18

346.73
Dol   Dolan, Edward F.
        Animal rights

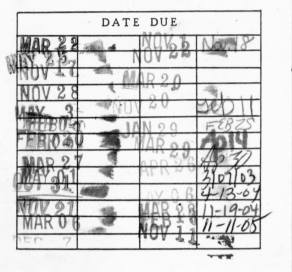

DATE DUE		
MAR 22	NOV 22	Nov 18
MAY 17	NOV 22	
NOV 17	MAR 20	
NOV 28	20	
MAY 3	NOV 20	SEP 11
FEB 02	JAN 29	FEB 25
FEB 20	MAR 29	2014
MAR 27	APR 26	
MAY 01		3/07/03
		4-13-04
NOV 21	MAR 28	11-19-04
MAR 06	NOV 11	11-11-05
DEC 7		

163   87